TREASURE HUNTING
PAYS OFF!

Ram Publications

Complete Book of Competition Treasure Hunting (The)
    Learn the INSIDE FACTS and you, too, can become a WINNER.

Complete VLF-TR Metal Detector Handbook (The)
    THE OPERATIONAL/TECHNICAL MANUAL... thoroughly explains VLF/TR metal/mineral detectors and HOW TO USE them. Compares VLF/TR's with all other types.

Detector Owner's Field Manual
    The world's most complete field guide. Explains the total capabilities and HOW TO USE procedures of all types of metal detectors.

Electronic Prospecting
    Learn how to find gold and silver veins, pockets, and nuggets using easy electronic metal detector methods.

Gold Panning Is Easy
    This excellent field guide shows you how to FIND and PAN gold as quickly and easily as a professional.

"How to Test" Detector Field Guide
    Learn how to find QUALITY before you buy... BFO, TR, VLF/TR, and discriminators.

Journals of El Dorado (The)
    The most misunderstood treasure hunting book. An invaluable research tool. Study this book and FIND TREASURE.

Professional Treasure Hunter
    Discover how to succeed with PROFESSIONAL METHODS, PERSISTENCE, and HARD WORK.

Successful Coin Hunting.
    The world's most authoritative guide to FINDING VALUABLE COINS with all types of metal detectors. The name speaks for itself!

Treasure Hunter's Manual #6
    Quickly guides the inexperienced beginner through the mysteries of FULL TIME TREASURE HUNTING.

Treasure Hunter's Manual #7
    The classic! THE book on professional methods of RESEARCH, RECOVERY, and DISPOSITION of treasures found.

Treasure Hunting Pays Off!
    An excellent introduction to all facets of treasure hunting.

By CHARLES GARRETT
Successful Coin Hunting
Treasure Hunting Pays Off!
Electronic Prospecting (with Lagal, Grant)
The Complete VLF-TR Metal Detector Handbook (with Lagal)

TREASURE HUNTING
PAYS OFF!

by

CHARLES GARRETT

A RAM GUIDEBOOK B. J. Nelson, Editor

ISBN 0-915920-37-9
Library of Congress Catalog Card No. 76-11375
© Copyright 1976
© Copyright rev. 1978 ed.
© Copyright 1980
  by Charles L. Garrett

PORTIONS OF THIS BOOK MAY BE REPRODUCED. All rights reserved except permission is granted to reproduce printed text and/or illustrations, not to exceed the equivalent of one chapter, provided the book title is included, full credit is given to the author, and the name and address of the publisher are given. For use of matter to exceed that amount, or to reproduce the book in series form it will be necessary to secure specific written permission from the publisher. Address all inquiries to Ram Publishing Company.

First Printing July 1976. Fifth printing August 1980. 15044/880

Printed in U.S.A. by
Yaquinto Printing Co., Inc. • 4809 S. Westmoreland • Dallas, Texas 75237

For FREE listing of related treasure hunting books write
Ram Publishing Company • P.O. Drawer 38649 • Dallas, Texas 75238

CONTENTS

I	Discover the Real Meaning of Treasure	1
II	What's It All About?	3
III	Let's Go Treasure Hunting	7
IV	Research? It's Actually Fun and Rewarding!	11
V	Successful Treasure Hunting with a Metal Detector	13
VI	Treasure Is There To Be Found!	17
VII	Let's Go Coin Hunting!	19
VIII	Let's Explore a Ghost Town for Relics, Caches and Bottle Dumps	27
IX	The 20th Century Gold Rush!	35
X	Searching for Battlefield Relics	47
XI	Lost Treasure on the Beach!	51
XII	It Is Easy To Understand Metal Detectors	53
XIII	Laws About Treasure Hunting	71
XIV	Conclusion	73
	Metal Detector Dealers	76
	Recommended Supplementary Books	80

Editor's Note

Charles Garrett, an active adventurer in God's great outdoors for 35-plus years, grew up exploring the deep East Texas Piney Woods. Following high school and four years' Navy duty during the Korean conflict, he attended Lamar State College of Technology in Beaumont, Texas, receiving his Bachelor of Science degree in Electrical Engineering. He spent the next eight years at Texas Instruments and Teledyne Geotech working with radar, earth sciences and Army metal detection instrumentation. In the mid-sixties Mr. and Mrs. Garrett founded Garrett Electronics.

Mr. Garrett devotes full time to developing, testing and producing metal/mineral detection equipment for the man in the field. He is conscientious and particularly well-qualified in these efforts not only because he works with fellow treasure hunters world-wide but also because he uses and depends upon his own equipment. His wide experience in electronics, military and earth sciences, together with his love and concern for his fellow man, has prompted him to share the results of his experiences unselfishly with all.

He has written numerous articles about treasure hunting, prospecting, and other outdoor adventuring. Other Ram books by Charles Garrett include *Successful Coin Hunting*, *Treasure Hunting Secrets* (a short, beginner's guidebook), *The Complete VLF-TR Metal Detector Handbook* (with Roy Lagal), and *Electronic Prospecting* (with Roy Lagal and Bob Grant).

CHAPTER I

Discover the Real Meaning of Treasure Hunting

You may be completely new to the field of Treasure Hunting, or you may have a lifetime of experience. Whatever your status, one thing is certain: if you don't know it now you soon will know that treasure hunting is an extremely interesting and rewarding hobby. Rewards come not only from the wealth you can discover, but also from the enjoyment of being in the vast outdoors. Treasure hunting will give you the "excuse" you may have been needing to get outside and enjoy this great land to its fullest. Treasure hunting (TH-ing) is a healthful activity that will reward you both physically and mentally. If you have a family, I strongly encourage you to let the whole family participate in your activities. Treasure hunting is a fine hobby that lets all family members, regardless of age, share in the many rewards.

When you become a Treasure Hunter, you will greatly expand your horizons in history and the study of people. You will also find yourself involved in many other interesting and rewarding hobbies, such as coin hunting and collecting; searching for lost money caches; ghostowning for "post hole banks," rare relics, and valuable bottles. You will find yourself involved in the many aspects of recreational mining, such as nugget hunting, electronic prospecting, mine searching, and searching for precious metal ore samples at mine dumps and tailings. Metal detecting even goes hand in hand with gold panning and dredging. All these things are great fun, worthwhile, and, believe me, well within your reach.

Of course, this guide is by no means complete. It never could be. Treasure hunting is a hobby that is expanding in many directions at a fantastic rate. It will lead you into areas you never dreamed of, and no other hobby is so truly American since every phase of TH-ing puts you in touch with our American past. You will learn laws you need to know and you will realize that Uncle Sam considers treasure hunting a very real and businesslike activity. Because treasure hunting has so many varied aspects I have received permission from Roy Lagal and Karl von Mueller to present some of the valuable information from their TH-ing books here. These men are two of the greatest, lifelong TH-ers you would ever meet and their books and TH-ing activities are known worldwide. You'll enjoy learning from them.

Mr. and Mrs. Wayne Cummings of Davenport, Iowa, have found all these and many more valuables with their metal detectors. Their finds are made in parks, playgrounds, and other areas where people congregate; however, many of their finds also have been made in shallow water to depths of thirty inches. Through research they locate old swimming areas, and then use their detectors underwater to locate valuables that swimmers have lost. This picture was taken in the Garrett Electronics museum. All of the items on display were found by treasure hunters. Admission to the museum is free to anyone who would like to come by and browse around. Museum address: 2814 National Drive, Garland, Texas (near Dallas).

CHAPTER II

What's It All About?

Treasure hunting is the searching for and recovery of an endless list of valuables. Lost coins, hidden money and jewelry, relics, bottle dumps and precious ore such as gold and silver veins and nuggets... these are but a few of the many things of value TH-ers are finding. There is no end in sight. People are even finding good use for things that only yesterday were considered trash. Every day new places are being found where valuables can be discovered. New and improved metal detectors allow the TH-er much greater efficiency and a wider range of TH-ing capabilities.

WHO TREASURE HUNTS?

TH-ing is becoming more and more a family hobby. Both husbands and wives quickly become avid TH-ers. Possibly fifty percent of today's coin hunters are women. Some children even become better TH-ers than their parents. More and more

Several years ago when this family went on their first coin hunting expedition they found a few coins around this old house. By coin hunting a few hours every weekend during the past two or three years this family could have accumulated from ten to fifteen thousand or more coins and other valuables.

campers, hunters, fishermen, vacationers and back-packers are adding detecting equipment to their sports gear. An advantage to treasure hunting is that it is neither a seasonal thing nor a one-person operation. For the family which enjoys doing things together this hobby could be the answer. There is great joy in planning a family treasure hunt, researching clues, taking notes, going over maps and other documents and then—making the recovery!

TREASURE HUNTING IS HEALTHFUL

Probably the most important benefit derived from treasure hunting is the health benefit. Treasure hunting takes you out of doors into the fresh air and sunshine. Scanning a detector over the ground all day, digging hundreds of holes, hiking several miles over the desert or climbing a mountain in order to reach a ghost town can become tiring. But, this is where an extra added benefit is realized. A "built-in" body building program is a valuable side benefit of TH-ing. Leg muscles firm up, flab around the middle begins to diminish as excess pounds drop off, breathing improves and nights of restful sleep result. Good physical exercise is required in treasure hunting and it can only lead to a longer, healthier life. It is good to combine a health-building program with an enjoyable hobby.

You may travel more than you probably imagine now and this travel, plus treasure research and related activities, will broaden your horizons and provide you with much mental stimulation.

TREASURE HUNTING IS PROFITABLE

TH-ing is profitable, simple and easy. Consider the hobby of coin hunting! The majority of all TH-ers begin their new hobby by coin hunting. Countless millions of coins have been lost and await recovery by the metal detector hobbyist. As you will learn later in this book, it is quite easy for a diligent coin hunter to find five thousand coins per year.

OTHER BENEFITS

Most important to many people is the awareness and enjoyment of the treasures of nature God has placed upon the earth for us all to find. Whether the "big money treasure" has been found is not always the point. It is truly gratifying to see nature in its purest form all around us and to be a vital part of it. This alone could well be the greatest "money" treasure ever found.

The educational factors related to treasure hunting are equally stimulating. From the relics and artifacts of bygone eras come many questions. Who were the people who once lived and prospered where only faint memories of a city or old lum-

The usage of metal detectors extends into many fields. Here Roy Lagal, Lewiston, Idaho, searches with a detector for gold nuggets in an Idaho mountain stream. Roy is extremely well-versed in the use of detectors not only in the field of prospecting but also in the areas of coin, cache and relic hunting. He is the author of several books about metal detectors and treasure hunting.

ber town remain? Where did they come from? Why was the area deserted? These and many more questions can usually be answered with proper research and examination of the artifacts found.

PROSPECTING FOR PRECIOUS METALS

The "pick and shovel" gold and silver mining areas of the 1800's are now rewarding today's metal-detecting prospector. Nugget hunting, prospecting, mine and ore vein searching, ore sample identification at mine tailings are all proving to be profitable. This is especially so because of the recent rapid rise of the value of gold and silver.

OTHER REWARDING TH-ING HOBBIES

TH-ing for other valuable items is very profitable and rewarding. Many persons who begin with coin hunting quickly extend their hobby into other areas of TH-ing. Searching ghost towns (and old houses) for hidden money caches, relics and rare bottles can be very rewarding. One TH-er found $41,000 in currency in a metal box that was cached in an old dumping ground. Another man found fifty, 100-year-old rifles buried beneath an old building. A man in Idaho found a $20 gold piece estimated to be worth many thousands of dollars. Hundreds of small fruit jar and "post hole" money caches are found each year. The truth is, a large army of TH-ers would have to work many years in order to reduce substantially the quantity of wealth which is awaiting the metal detector operator.

LET THIS BOOK BE YOUR GUIDE

This book should become your basic guide to *SUCCESSFUL TREASURE HUNTING*. It presents for your easy reading the basic aspects of TH-ing and metal detector types and applications. Many tips on where to search for the various kinds of treasure are given. Valuable information explaining not only where but how to search will be found throughout the book. And, a thorough reading will give you the knowledge you require in order to select the right kind of detector, the one best suited for your needs. A description of the best in TH-ing books by Ram Publishing Company is included for your convenience.

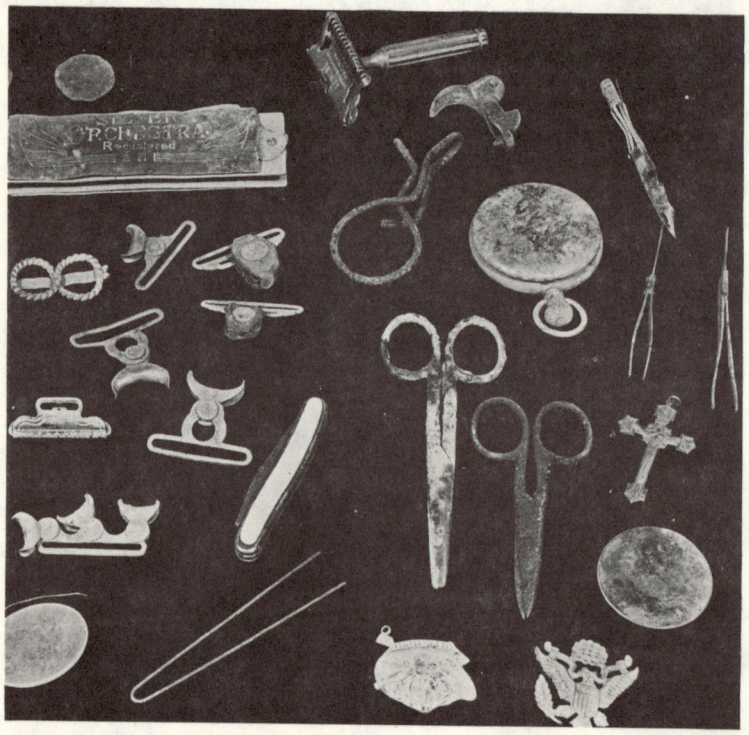

These are a few of the odds-and-ends relics found by Gene Rolls of Forest Ranch, California. Gene is an active treasure hunter who specializes in coin hunting and searching ghost towns. Note the harmonica, safety razor and watch. Relics like these demand high prices on the collectors' market. Photo by Roy Rolls.

CHAPTER III

Let's Go Treasure Hunting

COIN HUNTING MOST POPULAR

Coins are lost just about everywhere and most of them are easily found. Therefore, coin hunting is the most common form of TH-ing today. When a TH-er learns the most likely places to look for coins, he never comes home without his pockets bulging with coins which may date as far back as the time of the Romans and the Egyptians!

Quite often as the TH-er searches for treasure, he will locate many other things which can be converted into cash. Articles of bygone days will always demand a good price. Relics, such as guns and knives, are quite frequently found. War relics are demanding high prices today and most battle areas of the War Between the States are as yet almost untouched by the modern-day TH-er. These areas should be thoroughly searched for souvenirs of our historic past. The more a TH-er searches for and finds treasure, the more he will come to realize that there is a vast fortune awaiting anyone who diligently searches for it.

THINGS YOU MAY NEED
WHEN YOU GO TREASURE HUNTING

In the beginning you will need such basic items as a metal detector, a hunting knife for digging and probing, a small shovel, food, and drinking water. It is always a good idea to wear a hat and boots. As you gain experience you will add to and delete items from your detecting equipment.

WHAT ARE THOSE TOPOGRAPHICAL MAPS?

The United States Geological Survey is making a series of topographic maps to cover the United States, Puerto Rico, and the Virgin Islands. Maps are published which readily show cisterns, wells, houses, and other small landmarks. Cultural features such as roads, railroads, cities, and towns are shown, as well as features of relief such as hills, mountains and valleys. These maps are an absolute necessity in treasure hunting. They are ideal for the beginning treasure hunter because from these maps hundreds of possible treasure sites can be located within a few square miles of the TH-er's home. Most people, when they first see these maps, are surprised at the large number of abandoned houses and buildings which are located in their immediate vicinity. Buildings which are occupied are shown as small shaded squares. Buildings not occupied are square outlines which are not shaded. All known cisterns and wells are shown as small circles. A day or a weekend outing can be planned from these maps. Complete information concerning these maps may be obtained by writing to one of the following addresses: (areas east of the Mississippi) Distribution Section, U. S. Geological Survey, 1200 S. Eads, Arlington, Virginia 22202; (areas west of the Mississippi) Distribution Section Central Region, U.S.G.S., Box 25286, Denver Federal Center, Denver, Colorado 80225.

IS A METAL DETECTOR NEEDED TO FIND LOST OR BURIED TREASURE?

No, at least not treasure on the surface or in plain view of the eye, but ... what about the treasure that is hidden between the walls of an abandoned house or shack or maybe in the bricks of an old well? Unless you have been reliably informed, you will no doubt spend countless hours tearing away at boards or bricks to get to your treasure. Perhaps there was a legend of buried treasure on a certain parcel of land and through research you were able to narrow it down to one or two areas. Have you ever stopped to think how long it would take to turn over a

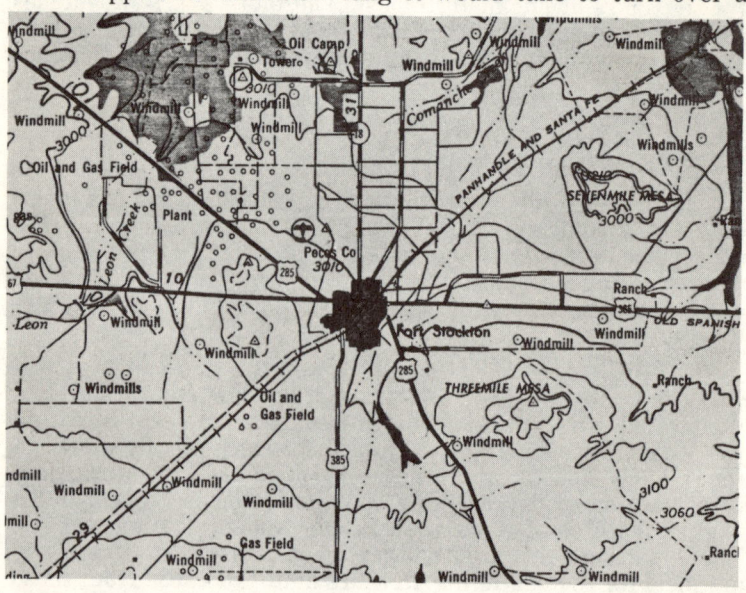

This picturegraphic map scale is 1: 250,000. Larger scales are available which show houses, barns, buildings, windmills, and man-made objects such as small cisterns and wells. It is easy to plan a day's outing by studying a topo map of any area.

hundred square feet of soil to a depth of several feet? What if, by chance, you discover an old homesite which may have the appearance of having once been a splendid home? How would you really go about recovering buried things from a by-gone era? Surely past generations have left things on the surface but for everything that you can see, think of all the things that lie beneath the surface!

So, is a metal detector really needed? I think you can answer that question more easily now. Your eyes are good, but let's also employ another type of "seeing"—electronic eyes —which can "see" not only through dirt, rock, water and wood, but will actually "talk" to you and "tell" you—"STOP! There is something here!" Valuable? Maybe, but regardless of the value you have recovered something that, without the aid of your detector, might have been left for others to find. Whether you are a professional treasure hunter or a weekend hobbyist, there is always a thrill when the steady hum of a detector speeds up to a fast tempo and the suspense of what is below grows until you bring the object to the surface!

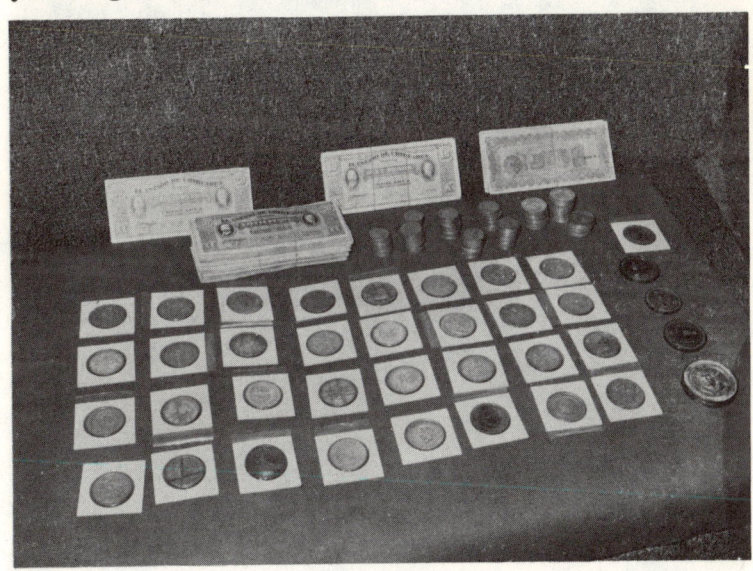

One lucky treasure hunter was searching an adobe ruins. He went inside one of the rooms. He scanned with his detector in the first corner . . . the second . . . the third . . . and finally, the fourth. His detector sang out loudly alerting the treasure hunter to the presence of something buried beneath the ground. Upon digging, he uncovered an old butter churn that was filled with these coins, medallions and currency. The currency was wrapped and waxed and preserved in "new" condition. The currency is Mexican, dated 1917. Perhaps this cache was put down during the time of Pancho Villa and the owner never returned to recover it. Metal detectors are a valuable aid to the treasure hunter. In fact, millions in lost treasure can be found only with detectors.

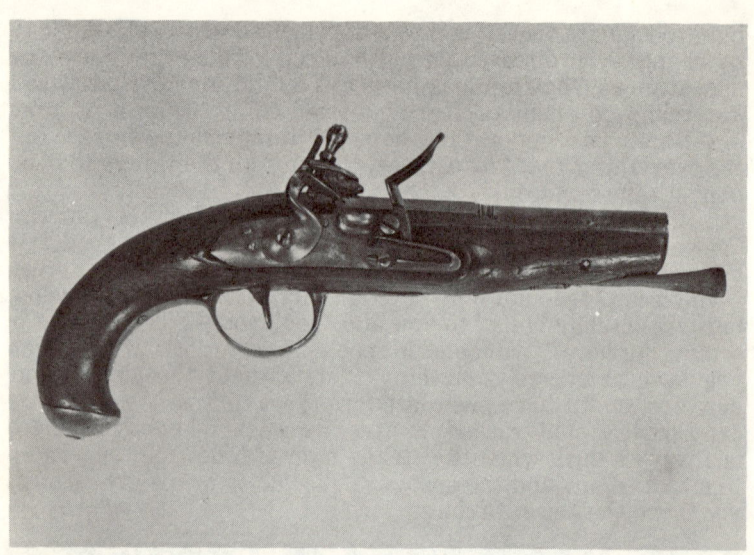

The flintlock pistol shown in the top picture was found by "Abe" Lincoln. He found the gun in an old building ruins in New Mexico. The gun was wrapped and protected so that it was preserved in almost-new condition. Along with the gun he found other valuables. The gun shown in the lower picture was found by Stanley Frank of Natchez, Louisiana. The weapon is on display in the Frank Museum in Natchez. Mr. and Mrs. Frank have been treasure hunting and searching States War battlefield sites for many years. They have amassed a tremendous collection of relics. Anytime you are in Central Louisiana, do not fail to go by to visit the Frank museum. You will always be welcome.

CHAPTER IV

Research? It's Actually Fun and Rewarding!

A vital key to successful treasure hunting is to find good places to coin hunt or locations where people have buried or hidden their money. Except for those locations sometimes discovered by accident, 90% of the time the success of a treasure hunt depends on careful research. You should learn how to research treasure leads and stories. Two of the best books on this subject are the *TREASURE HUNTER'S MANUALS #6* and *#7* by Karl von Mueller. He has spent a lifetime doing treasure research and he tells you how in these books. If you are interested primarily in coin hunting, my book, *SUCCESSFUL COIN HUNTING*, contains a great amount of information to help you find the best coin hunting areas.

When coin hunting, you will find that it takes a good day's work to search an acre of ground thoroughly with a metal detector. However, good research and a knowledge of human nature will allow you to find the most likely spots to be searched. If you are coin hunting in parks, look around the swings, slides, teeter-totters, merry-go-rounds, picnic tables and under trees where people often relaxed in the shade. While you will find coins wherever people have been, you should strive to find the oldest and probably the most rewarding coin hunting sites. This is one of the great secrets of coin hunting.

When searching for a suspected cache of money, remember this basic rule: whoever hid the money to begin with had to have landmarks to guide him back to the hiding place. Fence rows provide likely markers, as do old trees, large unusual rocks, or outcroppings of stone. One favorite method of marking a cache was to drive a nail on the underside of a tree limb, well away from the tree trunk. When it came time to dig up the cache, a weighted string was tied to the nail to mark the spot on the ground where the money was buried. Since the normal growth or shifting of most tree limbs is only a matter of inches during a lifetime, the system was reasonably accurate. Of course, in the olden days people who buried their money in such a fashion had no way of knowing that metal detectors would be invented! And that's where you come in! These persons have passed on, leaving their treasure to be searched out by the modern-day metal detector operator.

Still another popular place for burying money was in the chicken house. Chickens serve as excellent burglar alarms as they are likely to raise quite a noise when disturbed. Caches are often located between two points, such as half-way between two trees or somewhere along the "line" between the house and the well. An excellent method of determining where money might be buried is to put yourself in the shoes of the person who hid it originally and try to think like he or she did.

Leads can come from many sources. Reading current newspapers can often provide leads, as can reading old newspapers stored at libraries. A news story concerning the death of a wealthy man with no surviving heirs could easily lead a TH-er to some buried or hidden money.

Old-timers who can be found in every city and town may provide many valuable treasure leads. Talk to them. During the early years of their lives they knew a lot about where people gathered and which people had money. And, most of these old-timers love to reminisce about earlier days.

After you obtain treasure leads you must research all that is known about the story. Since no two treasure stories are exactly alike, you must use your own intelligence to get the information you need. However, there are some good guidelines on where to look for this information. Consider historical society records, old-timers, and newspapers. Records kept by city, county, state, and federal governments are public records, and you have a right to look at them. A check of the county surveyor's office may direct you to the site of a long-forgotten building which may be the focal point of your treasure lead. Reports filed long ago by the county sheriff may cast new light on the circumstances of a crime where money was never recovered. Here again, your expanding experience as a treasure hunter will allow you to sift through the information to sort out the important facts that could bring you closer to your big find.

CHAPTER V

Successful Treasure Hunting With a Metal Detector

A metal detector is an absolute must in Successful Treasure Hunting. Only armchair treasure hunting can be accomplished without a metal detector. How successful a treasure hunter is depends to a very large extent upon how well he has mastered his equipment. An expert using the poorest metal detector on the market will do better and find more buried and hidden objects than will an inexperienced TH-er who is using the best possible detector. In short, the TH-er must learn to use his detector correctly.

There are basically three types of detectors in which the hobbyist and treasure hunter will be interested: the BFO, the TR and the VLF. These instruments, when of quality construction and correctly used, will do their job. The BFO is an all-purpose metal/mineral detector capable of performing well regardless of the treasure hunting task. The "quick response" of the TR is one of the reasons for its popularity as a coin hunting detector. The VLF type detector is the deepest-seeking metal detector built. It has the ability to cancel negative (magnetic iron) ground minerals, giving almost perfect operation and great depth over even the worst soil conditions.

Discriminating circuitry can be installed in most detectors. This circuitry has the ability to reject most junk items, such as bottlecaps, tinfoil, and pulltabs, which unfortunately litter many of the public places where coin hunters like to search. In the past, the discrimination capability was available only by buying a detector specifically designed and constructed to perform this particular function. However, with the introduction of Garrett Electronics' new line of Hybrid Twin Circuit BFO and TR detectors, all operators now have their choice of both normal and discriminating circuitry in the same detector. On most models the discrimination feature can be switched off and non-discrimination switched in. This is very important because at old historical sites where every piece of metal, even iron, could have value and importance discrimination is not recommended as some items (an old gun, say) would be "rejected" by the discriminator. This dual feature gives the operator complete control over any TH-ing situation.

The TH-er should purchase the type of detector which is best suited to meet his requirements. It cannot be overemphasized that the TH-er must learn to use his instrument correctly.

Bob Podhrasky, Garrett Electronics' Chief Engineer, displays the company's four detector types. The VLF/TR Deepseeker, on the left, is the deepest seeking type instrument built. Next, the VLF/TR Featherweight "Groundhog" detector has rapidly become the coin hunter's favorite instrument, being outperformed in depth only by the Deepseeker models. Since the majority of the United States contains ground mineralization, Treasure Hunters have found these types of instruments to be their choice for extra deep hunting of coins, caches, and battlefield relics. The TR, second from the right, makes an excellent coin hunting detector for those who do not require ground canceling and extra deep depth. The BFO (right) has long been the favorite of Treasure Hunters who required ease of operation and all purpose uses. The newer VLF/TR types, however, have become the choice of many former BFO operators.

The detector instruction manual should be read thoroughly before operation of the detector is attempted. The operator should practice with his detector and use it exactly as the manufacturer has instructed.

Since metal detectors are the treasure hunter's most valuable tools, let's take a little more time here to try to understand them better.

VLF/TR DEEPSEEKERS

ADVANTAGES: Extreme Depth, particularly in the VLF ground canceling mode, readily detecting deeper than air tests. Universal capabilities, especially A•D•S• models, include SUPER DEPTH and unparalleled performance in CACHE, COIN and RELIC HUNTING and PROSPECTING.

DISADVANTAGES: Excessive trash (nails, etc.) may present problems, but if super-sensitivity is desired, some junk must be dug. TR mode produces excellent depth, even with full discrimination, but mineralized ground operation requires extra skill.

VLF/TR FEATHERWEIGHT "GROUNDHOG"

ADVANTAGES: Offers SUPERIOR COIN HUNTING DETECTION! Outstanding performance in TR Discriminate mode. Lightweight, compact, A•D•S• models. Universal capabilities include CACHE and RELIC HUNTING and PROSPECTING using a combination of both VLF and TR modes.

DISADVANTAGES: Less depth in VLF ground canceling mode when compared to Deepseeker. Heavy mineralization causes TR operating difficulty. Overcome with correct usage and understanding of controls.

TR'S

ADVANTAGES: TR's are excellent for coin hunting if you do not want the VLF's super-depth and mineral-free operation. Correctly designed discriminating TR's with Push Button Tuning are easy to use and their lower cost makes them popular coin hunting detectors.

DISADVANTAGES: The TR's operating characteristics make them difficult to operate over highly mineralized soil. Not recommended for Cache and Relic Hunting and Prospecting.

BFO'S

ADVANTAGES: Good performance in all phases of treasure hunting. Excellent discrimination capabilities. Reasonable performance over iron mineralized soil.

DISADVANTAGES: Definitely not as sensitive as other series. The greater the ground mineralization, the greater the difficulty in operating the BFO. No push button necessitates greater control manipulation.

YOU SHOULD KNOW WHAT YOU NEED

It is very important for you to have a basic understanding of the various types of detectors before investing your money. Search out responsible metal detector suppliers or write directly to detector manufacturers and request information. In addition to the Ram Publishing Company books already mentioned, there are other books that will help you learn a lot more about your chosen hobby.

In purchasing your first metal detector, you should shop for quality, as well as price. A poor quality metal detector that often fails to work or gives false signals over wet grass or weeds and other conditions because of poor design can be worse than no detector at all. You will be discouraged and perhaps turned away from a hobby that is truly fascinating and exciting. The selection and use of your metal detector is very important.

Let's review the important points. Select the type detector you really need (BFO, TR and VLF type) and make certain it is of good quality construction. Learn to use your detector properly. Carefully read the manufacturer's instruction manual and understand the instructions for operating the detector before attempting to use it. And finally, get out in the field and practice as much as you can, as often as you can. Soon your ear will become "tuned in" to your detector and its characteristic sounds, and you will become successfully involved in one of the most interesting and profitable hobbies imaginable.

CHAPTER VI

Treasure Is There To Be Found!

The word "treasure" is difficult to define. For all practical purposes, "treasure" may be anything that has a cash or convertible value. Treasure is usually thought of as a pirate's chest filled with doubloons, an outlaw's quickly-stashed bank loot, or at least an old iron pot filled with gold coins buried somewhere and forgotten. Interestingly enough, however, "treasure" to one person may be "trash" to another.

A junk box in an old barn may disclose a beautiful ornate glass lamp, or old letters to loved ones dating from the Indian territorial era. One treasure hunter found a powder horn beside a fully loaded and cocked Hopkins and Allen pistol under the front porch of an abandoned homestead in Oklahoma. Who can guess why it came to be there!

Many writers for adventure and treasure magazines have been inclined to distort or exaggerate the true treasure picture, even to the extent that many readers believe that few, if any,

Mrs. Harold McCorkell is an avid coin hunter. She searches primarily for coins and other small jewelry lost in parks, playgrounds and where people have gathered. One day while searching in an old park area her detector produced a loud signal indicating a large buried object. She thought, "Surely this is an old tin can," and passed on by the object. Later, after thinking about the signal she had received, she returned to the area and dug the object. This necklace is that object. It is an extremely rare and valuable Florentine necklace. One of the joys of treasure hunting is that you never know what you'll dig up next.

treasures exist that are worth less than thousands of dollars. Nothing could be further from the truth! Money in all forms, jewelry, guns, gems, heirlooms, genuine antiques, rare letters and stamps, documents (especially those bearing signatures of well-known people), rare and scarce books, securities, bullion, bottles, fruit jars and other glass containers, insulators and watches represent but a sampling of the rich harvest awaiting those who diligently search for treasure. These and countless more articles are certainly not in the "thousand dollar" category, but the finder will quickly learn that they rank high in collectors' markets.

The learned treasure hunter, however, goes into the field with his eyes wide open, and if what he finds does not interest him he surely knows that it may be of value to someone else. Consequently, the find will be retrieved for later sale or swap. Many TH-ers attach a tall yarn for added mileage. The world of treasure hunting is not a tinker's hobby; it is a real and very much "alive" avocation. It offers a new life of adventure, as well as an awareness of our heritage in this great country.

THE TREASURE HUNTER IS...?

The answer to this question is ... "anyone." Treasure hunters are just people—individuals or families finding once again that they have something in common. Every weekend many thousands of treasure hunters flock to the countrysides, lakes, deserts, ghost towns and other special sites in search of precious metals, such as gold and silver, or relics and artifacts of yesteryear. The fever of the treasure hunter is perhaps equal to that of the early-day California miners whose human stampede for gold was the greatest individual and united effort ever made in the history of free men aspiring to the attainment of personal wealth.

Unlike many sports or hobbies, treasure hunting doesn't center solely on a certain age group or sex. It holds excitement in store for men, women or children, regardless of their age. Many students, housewives and retired people find treasure hunting an escape from the boredom of routine, as well as an interesting and rewarding hobby.

TREASURE IS EVERYWHERE

Many people simply refuse to believe that any treasure could be hidden in or near their own home towns or, for that matter, in their own yards! There is treasure lost, buried or hidden in every county and parish of these United States—and it is being found daily. There has been an increasing number of sizeable treasures found during the past few years as more treasure hunting enthusiasts have begun to use more scientific methods, such as metal detecting, in their efforts to locate treasures.

CHAPTER VII

Let's Go Coin Hunting!

(Portions of this coin hunting section have been reproduced from my book, *SUCCESSFUL COIN HUNTING.)*
Coin hunting is the searching for and retrieving of lost coins. Countless millions of coins have been lost and await recovery by the metal detector hobbyist. Thousands of Indianhead and Wheat pennies, Buffalo nickels, Barber dimes, Liberty and Washington quarters, Liberty Walking half-dollars, and many other types of coins are being recovered every day. And, it appears people are losing more coins today than the coin hunter is finding! Coins are lost everywhere people go; coins are being found everywhere people have been. These facts support the belief that this aspect of treasure hunting is one of the fastest-growing family hobbies in America.
The person not familiar with the hobby of coin hunting finds it difficult to believe that coins can be found. "Who loses coins?", they say. "Surely there are not enough lost coins to make it worthwhile to buy a metal detector to go out and spend time looking for them!" A fitting reply is ... any active and experienced coin hunter can find five thousand coins each year. This is only an average of 100 coins found each weekend for fifty weeks ... a reasonable and obtainable goal. On any given weekend an experienced coin hunter can find from 100 to 500 coins. However, this same person would not find any coins in this same length of time if he did not follow the rules he has learned in coin hunting. A coin hunter *must* search for coins where they are lost, and they are lost where people have been. It is easy after a short time to learn the best places to search for coins, and there are hundreds of "best places."
At the site of an old drive-in theater my father and I found more than 250 coins in an area eighteen feet square. We recovered these coins from the small area immediately in front of the projection booth in a period of less than ninety minutes. Around the perimeter of this area a pipe railing had been built to keep persons from walking in front of the projector lights. Apparently this railing drew kids like a magnet. They must have used it to climb on, swing on, tumble on, "ride horses" on, and for all other sorts of gymnastics. The majority of the coins were found beneath this fence and on both sides to approximately two feet out. Sometimes the coins came out in bunches in clumps of dirt. When I made the first sweep, the detector speaker went, "zip, zip, zip, zip, zip!" I thought, "There are

surely lots of pulltabs here." All of these "zips" were, however, money "zips."

This is just a typical example of the success which can be obtained by the coin hunter. Many coins commonly found in old areas are worth from several times their face value up to several dollars. Often the numismatic value of an occasional coin which the coin hunter retrieves can pay for a detector, with some left over! Occasionally, coins recovered are worth up to many thousands of dollars. And, don't forget the "value" in rediscovering a moment of the past. Each time a coin is lost a moment of life is preserved until someone finds that coin.

As you search for coins you will encounter coin hunting youngsters from age four to beyond age eighty. There is no age limit. Coin hunting is popular because it is fun and rewarding. Even though detectors have been around for many years, coin hunting has carved a notch for itself in the outdoor hobby world just during the last few years. Coin hunting, like treasure hunting, is becoming more and more a family hobby. Wives are becoming as avid coin and treasure hunters as husbands; and the children are beginning to join in! I have seen some young children who could find more coins than could their parents. Many people coin hunt for the fun of it, as well as for the relaxation and good exercise they get. It gives people something interesting to do. It not only is relaxing mentally and physically, but it is also rewarding in many other ways. More

The author searches for coins in a city park. This spot under the tree proved to be a good location because many coins were found. Apparently children used the tree to climb on and in so doing lost the coins. In searching parks or any other areas the detector operator should try to locate the most likely places where coins will be found.

This little girl tries to locate lost coins with her detector. People of all ages are finding that coin and treasure hunting are fun and rewarding. Metal detecting is a sport in which all family members can participate.

Wallace Chandler spends most of his free time searching for valuables that have been lost in swimming areas. He says that these areas prove to be most lucrative. This picture shows just a small quantity, yet a good representative sample, of the types of things he finds beneath the water. He built a specially-constructed shovel which has the blade welded 90 degrees from the handle axis. This "scoop" is all he needs to retrieve the objects he locates with his detectors.

and more campers, hunters, fishermen, vacationers, and backpackers are adding coin hunting instruments to their sports gear. They are finding that coin hunting is filling gaps in their regular sports and other outdoor activities, and it provides added enjoyment for all members of the family.

Where do coin hunters find coins? That's easy! Anywhere people have been—which is practically everywhere. Once a person has begun this hobby he will no longer need convincing that coins are to be found. The number of places to search is all but endless! New coin hunting locations turn up daily. People write telling me about new discoveries. I pick up many valuable leads from newspapers, club bulletins, and other publications written about people. Old-timers tell you of places you could never learn about from other sources. Use your head; think! For instance, I searched for years before I suddenly realized that coin hunters should be able to find coins under the clothesline. And, sure enough, they were there. You can easily prove to yourself that mothers are unable to completely remove all coins and metal objects from the pockets of their little boys' and husbands' clothes before washing and hanging them to dry.

Above all, don't make the mistake of believing there are no coins to be found where you live. If you don't have the experience now, you soon will gain the knowledge to convince yourself that coins are truly found everywhere. The first place every person should start searching is right in his own backyard, branching out from there. The reason for writing this paragraph is that I have encountered many people who told me there was nothing in their areas worth searching for! The truth is, it would take an army of thousands of coin hunters, working many years, to search and clean out all the productive areas in the United States.

No one can deny that there are tremendous quantities of coins awaiting the all-seeing "eye" of a metal detector. The only problem you, as a coin hunter, will have is deciding which of many places to search next! More than 500 places are listed in SUCCESSFUL COIN HUNTING, and to get you started here are a few of them:

your own backyard; in driveways; all around your house and sidewalks; around hitching posts, racks, mailboxes, bus stops, parking meters, ticket stands; under trees, clothesline poles, bridges, piers, bandstands, and stadium seats; at schools, churches, old buildings, drive-in theaters, and children's camps; at the beach, old ghost towns, parks, and community gathering places ... and don't forget fireplugs—dogs don't lose coins, but little children playing "leap the fireplug" do!

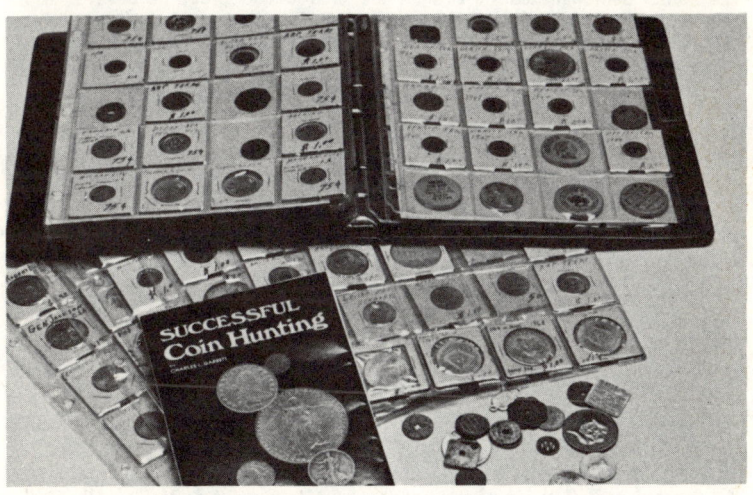

The owner of these coins and tokens has found an excellent way of cataloging and storing his finds. Since part of the fun of finding coins is identifying them and determining their value, all coin hunters should make it a habit to purchase one or more good books that identify and describe coins and give their values. Generally, all extra-valuable and rare coins should be protected and guarded against damage. The author's book, *Successful Coin Hunting*, devotes a chapter to the knowing, finding and keeping track of your coins. It also devotes a chapter to the care and protection of your coins.

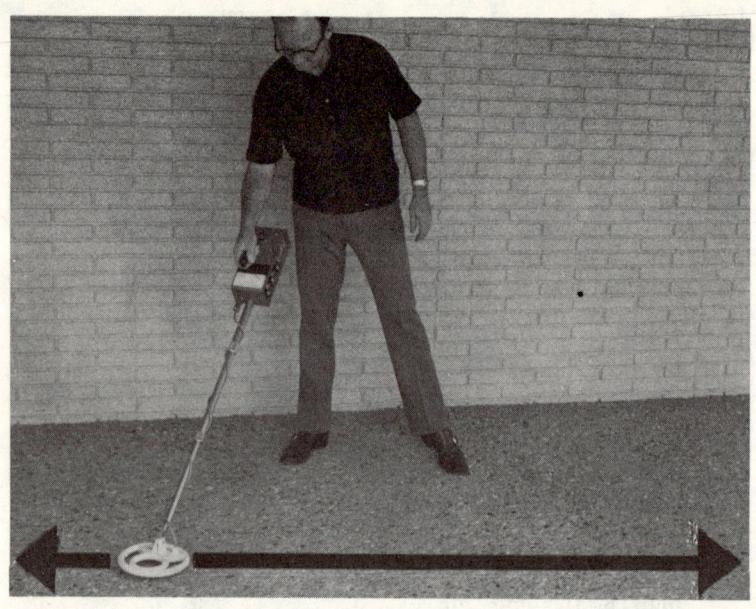

The author demonstrates the straight line, side-to-side sweep he believes is the best scanning method to use. More ground can be covered, and the coil can be kept at a constant height above the ground throughout the full sweep.

USE YOUR DETECTOR CORRECTLY

Sensitivity and correct searchcoil size for your detector are prime requisites to achieving success in coin hunting. If selecting a TR, you will generally have your choice of either a 6-inch or 8-inch diameter searchcoil. The 8-inch coil is by far the most popular TR coin hunting coil. It gives excellent depth, good scanning width, and good pinpointing. Place the searchcoil flat on the surface of the ground, adjusting the tuning until you hear a faint audio response. Move the searchcoil in a sidewise sweep in front of you, overlapping each sweep slightly to prevent missing any coins. Some operators like to tune the TR in the "null" or silent area, but the result is to lose part of the sensitivity, and there is the chance of missing deeper coins. Practice will be the deciding factor as to how the individual likes to set the tuning. It is not mandatory that you operate the TR searchcoil flat on the surface of the ground. You will, however, gain an inch or so of depth when the coil is scrubbed on the ground.

If you decide upon a BFO for coin hunting, select the 3½-inch, 5-inch, or 6½ inch searchcoil. The 3½-inch is best for beginners. The 5-inch and 6½-inch coils are the best all-around sizes, but some experience is required in order to get maximum depth from them. The operation of the all-purpose BFO detector differs slightly from that of the TR detector. The BFO searchcoil will probably operate best at approximately one-half to two inches above the surface of the ground, depending on ground mineral content. Set the tuning in the metallic mode of operation at a moderate speed. Some like a moderate motorboating sound; some like a faster sound. You will find the constant sound of the BFO audio variations slightly harder to distinguish than the quick response of the TR. With practice, however, you will be able to hear even the slightest increase in beats. BFO searchcoil choices include the 3½-inch and 6½-inch independently-operated dual coils. With these coils you may conduct your search with the larger coil, and then switch to the smaller coil to pinpoint a target. There are other advantages to the independently-operated dual coils, such as determining object size and depth and the convenience of being able to select various coil sizes rapidly with the flick of a switch.

The new ground canceling detectors (VLF and VLF/TR) have rapidly replaced TR and BFO detectors. The new ground canceling detectors are not bothered by most ground iron minerals and they produce super-depth, permitting the operator to successfully rework coin hunting areas that have been worked many times with less sensitive TR's and BFO's.

The VLF"s seven-to-eight inch searchcoils are the most popular. The larger searchcoils, however, should not be overlooked as very productive coin and treasure hunting coils. These larger coils (10½-inch, for example) produce great depth, and even though the diameter is larger than that of the smaller coins, pinpointing is very easy. You can get those extremely deep coins and rings and, with just a little practice, can pinpoint them exactly.

The author searches this West Texas ghost town with a Master Hunter VLF/TR Deepseeker detector. These VLF/TR type instruments are "Total Capability" instruments in that they will perform all phases of treasure hunting. They are as at home when ghost-towning as they are when called upon to coin hunt, cache hunt, prospect, nugget hunt, identify ore samples, and, in general treasure hunt. The days of carrying around several different types of detectors are over. The new VLF/TR's will do it all!

CHAPTER VIII

Let's Explore a Ghost Town for Relics, Caches and Bottle Dumps

EXPLORE A GHOST TOWN

A popular and rewarding hobby is "ghostowning." The word can cover a number of activities and a large variety of recovered items. You will discover old coins, perhaps a buried treasure cache, relics or antiques dating back to the Pilgrims or lost items from only yesterday. Any place people have gathered will produce relics or coins. There are thousands of abandoned town sites, old forts, homesteads and farmhouse locations. The list is endless. Finding a place to search will never be your problem ... only the time needed to pursue and enjoy your hobby. You will need a good metal/mineral detector for your search since most surface items have already been picked up, and those remaining will lie below the surface.

Ghostowning differs greatly from prospecting as a hobby. You may use any type of metal/mineral detector and achieve satisfactory results. The TR detector or the BFO will perform equally well in the search for small coins and relics.

Your choice will be determined by whether you like the semi-silent operation of the TR or the constant beating sound of the BFO. If you are thinking of purchasing one of the new discriminators that reject all items other than coins, you should consider the fact that a ghostowner will want to recover ALL metallic items. A non-discriminating detector should be used for this purpose.

After you have located a possible ghost town site, spot-check several areas to see if anything is there. It does not take much to confirm your location ... perhaps an old nail or some other meaningful object. Sweep the entire area with your searchcoil if you have time. Otherwise, choose the most likely-looking spots and pay close attention to both metal and mineral signals. Sometimes an old iron relic will deteriorate to the point where it may respond as mineral. It is returning to the natural state from which it came (magnetic iron mineral), and is simply oxidizing (or rusting).

A one-hundred-year-old rifle was found in Athens, Texas, by a treasure hunter who was curious enough to search the attic of an old house even though he had already thoroughly scanned the ceiling of the room below with his metal detector. He found the rifle leaning against a rafter, stock down. The wooden stock plus the thickness of the ceiling were enough to keep the detector from picking up the metal in the rifle.

A small velvet-lined box which held over $1,000-worth of goodies was found in an old two-story house in Colorado. The lucky treasure hunter who found it was working his way up an enclosed staircase with his metal detector when he got a reading from a spot in the wall about halfway up the stairs, a place where it didn't seem structurally logical for it to be. On the second floor he discovered a closet against the wall with a shelf directly over the spot where he had gotten the reading about nine feet below. The wall was open behind the shelf, and evidently the box with its tiny but valuable hoard had been accidentally knocked off the shelf, falling the nine feet until it lodged against a crossbeam.

Why didn't someone hear it fall from the shelf, or why didn't the owner miss it when moving out of the house? In all probability, the owner had died, and the heirs, friends, or relatives who cleaned out the house knew nothing about the box. They may even have heard it fall while clearing the closet shelf, but, for all they knew, it could have been an old shoe. Far from being a worthless old shoe, the box contained five $20 gold pieces, a heavy gold chain and necklace, a gold stickpin and a miniature toy pistol and holster.

Karl von Mueller, author and lifelong treasure hunter, tells of a straw-encased bottle filled with 773 dimes which was found with a metal detector near Maitland, Florida, over the doorway of an old shack. The find was made in 1960 but the coins were all dated prior to 1918. There were 46 of the rare 1916-D's, now worth about $100 each; two 1895-O's, each listed at about $50 on today's market; and ten 1904-S's, worth $10 apiece. The numismatic value of the others probably brought the total value of the cache to over $5,000. The most significant aspect of the find, however, is that when the coins were hidden they were probably worth little more than their face value of $77.30. In other words, they were probably not hidden by a wealthy person but rather, as the modest shack would indicate, by someone relatively poor. This bears out the old cliché that, "treasure is where you find it."

Books on the subject of "where to search" will help familiarize you with different areas. However, common sense and a good detector will generally take care of most of your problems. Few ghost town hunters come in empty-handed. The relics and old coins are there, just waiting to be found. Remember to leave the area as you found it—clean—and be sure to refill all holes. Use courtesy at all times; you might want to go back.

WHAT IS CACHE HUNTING?

Cache (pronounced "cash") hunting is seeking money or valuables that have been put away or cached by someone. The little old lady's "hard times" coins she buried in a jar in the

Karl von Mueller, author of the *Treasure Hunter's Manuals #6* and *#7* and co-author of the popular treasure research book, *The Journals of El Dorado*, is an acknowledged expert in all aspects of treasure hunting and prospecting. He writes with authority based upon long years of in-the-field experience. His books are "musts" for those interested in the fascinating world of treasure seeking and allied hobbies.

garden, the old man's bank jar he kept hidden in the bottom of a fence post hole, or the washtub filled with gold coins ... these are all "caches." There are many, many thousands of this type of treasure awaiting the detector operator who seeks them out. They are buried from only a few inches to arm's length under ground surface. If they are not dug up by the treasure hunter, they will stay buried forever. These treasures can be found anywhere: in the chicken coop; halfway between the well and a tree; between two trees; in the horse stall under the ground; in the walls of houses and barns and in countless other places.

To search for caches, the detector operator should use a 10-inch or larger diameter searchcoil. Of course, house or barn searching does not necessarily call for large coils. Since walls are only a few inches thick, even coils as small as 3½-inch can be used. These coils, do, however, detect small objects, such as nails, which larger coils may not detect. However, you should remember when searching staircases, attics (from the room below . . . even though this is not the recommended procedure) you may need the greater range that the larger coils give.

To search buildings for caches, do not use the discriminating capability of your detector unless you are looking only for precious metals. Many caches are buried in containers of iron and would be rejected by a detector which is being operated in the discrimination mode. Also, iron relics that are sometimes found in abundance in old houses and barns would likewise be rejected.

GO RELIC HUNTING

One of the most rewarding aspects of ghost town hunting is the recovery of relics. Usually ghost towns became deserted over a very short period of time and when the residents moved they often left behind things they simply did not have room to carry or pack. These items, such as tools, pieces of furniture, old trunks, kitchen utensils, old pictures and picture frames are very valuable to today's antique collectors and dealers. They are well worth recovering.

In searching out a ghost town try to visualize the layout of the town—where buildings once stood, or, if the buildings are still standing, try to locate the buildings which had very high traffic, for example, the general store, the post office, or the saloon. The locations and pathways between the buildings are excellent areas to search for relics and coins. If possible, go to a high hill or point and look at the old town site as a whole to get a better idea of traffic patterns through it. Search the most promising areas first, then work out the rest of the site as time allows. Once you become familiar with the life-style of the old town searching will begin to become second nature to you.

L. L. "Abe" Lincoln of Rogers, Arkansas, displays a few of his most valuable coins. Many of them are gold coins which he found while searching around one-hundred-year-old Idaho gold mining camps. Abe has been very successful in all phases of treasure hunting, and it is most rewarding to talk with him about his experiences. He will quickly tell you that the greatest virtue required in treasure hunting is patience combined with more patience.

When you have learned about your ghost town, you will probably return year after year, searching out new locations.

Every ghost town has a well-stocked supply of bottles and relics buried in its trash dump. If you can locate a dump site you will have an almost endless supply of bottles and relics to provide many summers of excitement and profit. Dump sites are not hard to find if you will use a good detector with a deep-seeking coil. As a general guide to where a dump site can be found, draw on your knowledge of human nature. Dump sites will almost always be located downwind from the town. Downwind means the dump would not smell up the town during the summer months when residents opened the windows of their homes. (No air-conditioning in those days!) Also, dumps are almost always located on the downhill side away from town for obvious reasons of sanitation. Once you have discovered one or more likely-looking sites, put your detector to work to try to locate the metal debris that is always present in dumps.

As you collect relics and mementos from the past, remember that almost everything old has a collectors' value or an interest value to someone. Retrieve all relics. Sooner or later you will find somebody who will want an item you had at first not considered worth the trouble. If, after a couple of years, you still don't want to keep it, get rid of it. You will be surprised, however, at how valuable some of your items will be.

After several successful relic hunts you will probably want to sell some of the items you have found. Two of the best places to sell your relics and antiques are flea markets and garage sales. Flea markets, if they have good publicity and high numbers of customers, are very profitable. A good display of relics and antiques and other collectibles has been known to produce over $200 in sales on a good-weather weekend. Also remember that most states do not charge sales tax on relics and antiques at flea markets since all of the items there are second-hand.

One more thing must be said about relics and antiques. They are two of the best investments known to man. It has been estimated that more money is invested in antiques than in the stock market. Antique investment is believed to be second only to real estate investment. Like real estate, the quantity of antiques is limited, but demand keeps growing at a rapid pace. One relic specialist, J. B. Estes, made the statement, "I will buy back every relic I have sold for the price paid. I could then resell the relic for at least twice as much as the first time."

FIND AND DIG A BOTTLE DUMP!

More and more collectors are turning to the metal/mineral detector to aid in the search for old bottle dumps. The great popularity of antique bottle collecting has reduced the number of easily identifiable dump areas and the number of digging spots. Some sort of tool or electronic device is needed to help locate the tin cans and other metallic items that generally abound in dump areas. The metal detector has proved to be the fastest and most practical aid.

The type of detector to use is not important, but you should use the larger searchcoils to gain extra depth. As a few dumps will be rather shallow, the standard 12-inch loop will be adequate, but most of the really old ones are deep. The larger searchcoils will be necessary, the larger the better, and you may recover some deep items missed by other searchers with smaller coils. Choose fully-shielded searchcoils to eliminate grass and weed interference. The all-purpose detectors will operate best under these search conditions, but you will have some degree of success no matter what detector or method you employ.

A ground probe is helpful to save needless digging. When a detector signal is received, insert the probe to try to define what or how deep the metal is. Sometimes there will be NO glass in a small trash dump, and by using the probe in conjunction with the metal detector you will save unnecessary work. With experience, you will know if your probe has touched

This man, Mr. J. B. Estes, is a very successful full-time treasure and coin hunter. During the week he searches for treasures and relics in ghost towns and old abandoned buildings. He rarely passes up a likely-looking park or playground in his quest for coins. On weekends he sets up shop at flea markets anywhere from California to Virginia. At these flea markets he sells the relics and many of the other valuables that he finds during the week. He is well-known throughout the circuit as the "Texas Trader." Look for him at your local flea markets. You'll probably find him. If you do, ask him the story behind any of the relics on his tables. You will then be rewarded with a fascinating tale of how he recovered the object in an old abandoned ghost town.

metal, wood, glass or rock.

Collectors interested primarily in antique bottles sometimes discover a treasure cache, so never abandon an area because there is evidence of digging and previous searches. It is almost impossible for any hunter to "clean" an area completely. Many areas that have produced good bottles are constantly being reworked by collectors using metal/mineral detectors. Areas searched many times are still producing. The detector will not replace the shovel and bottle rake but it can help find concealed dumps others have missed.

There are many good bottle books available to help you learn about and identify valuable bottles. Don't buy or sell bottles until you know their value!

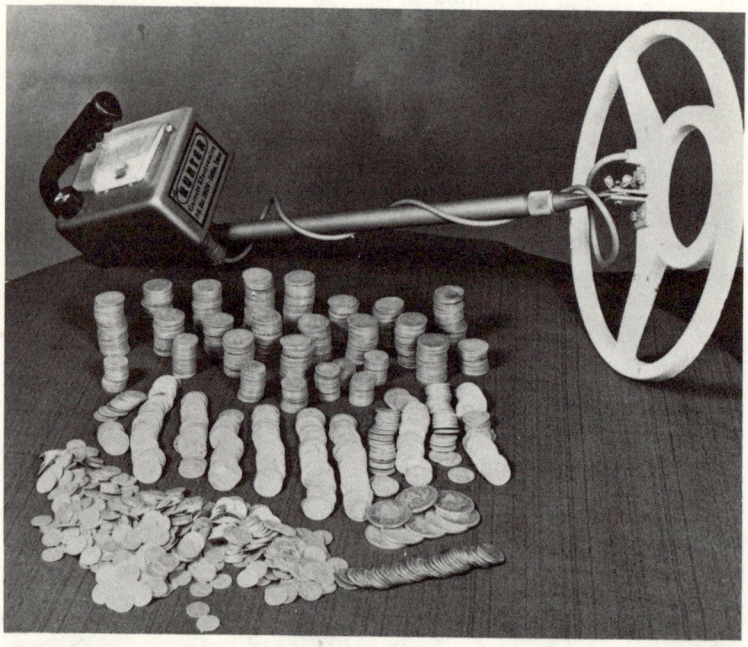

Bill Mason, Minnesota Prospector's Supply, is an avid treasure hunter. He has found many caches of coins and other valuables. In this picture you see some of the contents of several of his finds. This type of success requires long hours of research, patience, and effort. Make no mistake about it ... treasures are there to be found!

CHAPTER IX

The 20th Century Gold Rush!

On December 31, 1974, the United States Government ended its 41-year-old ban on the private ownership of gold. President Franklin Roosevelt had brought about this ban on gold ownership as one of the methods of shoring up the nation's economy. As December 31, 1974, drew near, foreign gold markets got ready to make large profits by selling gold to U.S. citizens, whom they thought were chomping at the bit to buy gold. As it turned out, it didn't happen that way. They did not realize that the gold rushes in the U. S. were made by Americans seeking FREE gold, not gold being sold at a very high market price. The adventuresome Americans who migrated to California in 1849 and again in 1859, then moved to Colorado in 1891, were not looking for the right to buy gold at high prices. They wanted to find the gold themselves and to make their own fortunes. Much of that same spirit can be found in the gold-producing areas of the United States even today. Gold is being recovered by treasure hunters who have discovered the pleasures and profits of week-end prospecting.

ELECTRONIC PROSPECTING

Had our early-day prospectors been equipped with today's metal/mineral detectors, today's gold rush might never have come about. Without question, the prospectors of 75, 100, and 125 years ago were knowledgeable and experienced in their profession. They recovered countless millions of dollars worth of gold, silver and other precious metals and minerals. They used every conceivable method to remove from reluctant Mother Earth every last ounce of the precious metals that they could find. Basically, however, they were limited in their searching to their eyesight. They could scour the country until they found likely-looking signs of gold. Then they would set about to pan the stream or dig into the mountainside—just wherever their eyes and their sixth sense would tell them to investigate. If things looked just right in some place in the stream, they would set up their gold recovery system and go to work.

To be sure, today's electronic prospector depends upon his eyes, but he also turns on the electronic "eyes" of his metal/mineral detector. He can scan not only likely-looking places, but he can also scan in areas and even under water (where the old prospector could not see) to locate black sand and gold deposits that might well have been physically impossible for his gold prospecting ancestors to locate. With today's detector even entire stream beds, wet or dry, can be quickly and efficiently scanned for minute traces of that precious stuff.

The hardrock miner had his limitation, too! He could chip and blast away deeper and deeper as he followed gold and silver veins, but, when the vein stopped, the miner stopped. Even though there might have been an even richer vein just inches away, the early-day miner couldn't see it. Today's electronic prospector can see it, however! The eyes of the modern metal/mineral detector can easily penetrate deeply into the walls of a mine to locate veins of precious metal.

It is estimated that there is more gold left in the ground than all the gold that has been taken out! Even if this statement is not true, sufficient quantities of precious metals are being found to prove that gold and silver are still waiting to be found. Elaborate mining equipment and a lifetime of experience are not needed. Today's modern electronic prospector equipped with a quality metal/mineral detector can find it. The information given in this book, plus sufficient research to locate yesterday's gold bearing regions, is all one needs to get started. On weekends and vacations the recreational miner can begin the search for his or her share of precious metal. Not everyone

The author searches in this abandoned mine for ore veins and pockets missed by early-day miners. Since these miners depended primarily upon their eyesight, they could not "see" the rich veins that might lie only a fraction of an inch beneath the surface of their mine tunnels and shafts. Both the VLF and BFO types of detectors can be used in mines, but the VLF will penetrate more deeply.

succeeds, however, and failure is probably due to two things: not searching in the correct places and/or not being patient enough. Success might be only a few flakes of gold panned from a stream or a few valuable ore specimens that the electronic eyes of the detector located in an old mine dump... or, it could be a rich ore vein of pure silver or gold.

YOU CAN FIND HIGH GRADE ORE

As you travel through the deserted gold fields you will see abandoned tunnels, rock heaps (called "tailings") and piles of ore that never made it to the stamp mill to be crushed. As you explore these areas, remember that mining of the earlier days was often by sight only. If you use your metal/mineral detector properly and thoroughly scan the rocks which are in these dumps, oftentimes you can recover good ore samples. Extreme caution should be exercised around deserted mines for several reasons. You do not necessarily have the right to enter and begin searching just because no one is around. If possible, gain permission. There are a lot of old-timers with valid claims who could possibly object to your doing a little "high grading". Another reason for caution is that of safety. Many old mine shafts have not had maintenance for many years. Be doubly cautious if there are wooden timbers used to shore up the ceiling since they probably have become rotted and are not really supporting the ceiling weight. Any loud sound or movement against the timbers or walls of a tunnel could bring the mountain down on top of you. You are advised NOT to lean over and peer down a mine shaft. Poisonous fumes coming up from such shafts have been known to instantly kill persons who only wanted to get a look at an old shaft.

If you find a good mine location and receive permission to search, begin by checking the floor with your metal/mineral detector. All the ore ever taken from the mine had to cross the tunnel floor, and it's almost certain some of it fell off the ore carriers and was eventually covered with other rocks and dirt. Also check out the walls and ceiling. Once again, remember the early miners had no metal detectors, and could have been only inches away from a vein of gold even larger than the one they were following when they dug the tunnel years ago.

If you live in the gold producing areas of the United States, or if you are planning a vacation to the gold country, recreational mining will prove to be one of the most satisfying experiences of your life. It will provide you with memories which will be talked about to your friends for years.

LET'S GO NUGGET HUNTING!

Old placer diggings and the bottoms of dry washes are the most productive and rewarding locations for nuggets. In remote desert areas where water has never been available and the only method of recovery is "dry panning," there are millions of dollars worth of small nuggets. The nuggets rarely are detectable by eyesight but they do lie almost on the surface or at very shallow depths. Investigation of low-lying areas with a highly sensitive metal/mineral detector can be very rewarding. Some knowledgeable nugget hunters have done quite well over the years by working dry or desert areas in highly mineralized locations. Use of the metal/mineral detector is practically the only method of locating these deposits. It is certainly one of the fastest.

Operate your searchcoil as closely to the ground as possible to receive the best indication on small nuggets and to gain a slight advantage in depth. A fast sweep will produce the best signal on these tiny objects. A slower movement would allow the background noise to be confused with the signal.

All detectors are *not* suitable for prospecting and poor results received with some detectors have simply caused the hobbyist to quit this interesting and profitable pursuit.

ROCKS, GEMS, MINERALS

The most important and useful tool of the rockhound (besides his rock hammer and patience) can be the metal/mineral detector. If it is properly understood and operated, its use can be very rewarding and interesting, but it should not be used as the ultimate answer to the positive identification of all minerals and gems. Nothing can replace knowledge gained from experience in the identification of semiprecious stones and gems. The metal/mineral detector should be used as an accessory to the rockhound's field equipment to aid in locating conductive metallic specimens that the human eye cannot distinguish or identify. Check known samples and become acquainted with the metal/mineral detector. You cannot see inside an ore specimen; a good quality VLF/TR or BFO can.

For identification purposes the metal/mineral detector defines "metal" as any metallic substance of a conductive nature in sufficient quantity to disturb the electromagnetic field of the searchcoil. Gold, silver, copper, and all the nonferrous metals are just that — *metals*. The only *mineral* that responds to the detector is magnetic iron, or iron oxide, chemically described as Fe_3O_4. If your detector responds to a target as "metallic," bring it in; it contains conductive metal in some form. If the detector responds as "mineral" it means only that the specimen contains more mineral than it does metal in a detectable form. As a result of a few minutes' work you might find some high grade metallic sample that has been passed over for years by fellow rockhounds.

Conduct bench tests to familiarize yourself with the response produced by both metal and mineral specimens you already know. This testing will aid greatly in future identification. When conducting your field searches, use the detector only as an aid, not as a complete searching tool. Test many rocks, for such testing will increase your knowledge and may help you find many valuable specimens. In the identification of mineral as opposed to metallic ores, the new VLF/TR and BFO detectors will produce better results than the TR. The TR detector tuned in the metal mode will give different signals on the same specimen of metallic ore, depending on which part of the searchcoil it touches. A large gold nugget placed on the receiver portion of the coil will produce a metal response. Placing it on the portion of the coil containing the transmitting coil causes a mineral, or negative, response, as will a small pebble of extremely high grade magnetic iron ore on the receiver coil. On the transmitting portion of the coil it will respond as positive, or metallic. Many rockhounds have turned from the TR detector because of unreliable identification of known ore specimens. This is not a failing of the detector but merely a function of its particular type of operation. Always use a quality detector with a 100% shielded searchcoil when testing ore samples as the entire surface of the coil will respond the same, either metallic or mineral, and lessen the chances of false identification.

When searching for gems or high grade specimens of metallic ore, pay close attention to old mine tailings. You may find that "worked out" area isn't so barren, after all. Certain gems, such as the thunder-egg, have a covering of outside magnetic iron. Some forms of jade and even garnet respond to the mineral side of a good VLF/TR or BFO detector.

HOW TO LOCATE BLACK SAND POCKETS

Concentrations of black sand do not necessarily contain gold but, since magnetic sand is heavy and gold is heavier, tend to stop in nature's "sluice boxes" (small cracks and crevices into which gold can fall and become lodged). Notice when you operate your gold pan that the black sand also traps behind the riffles. It is the same with nature's "sluice boxes." Locating these black sand pockets with a metal/mineral detector is possible, both underwater and on dry land.

Your choice of detector should be the new VLF/TR or BFO. For underwater searches for black sand pockets the choice of searchcoil sizes should be governed by the bottom of the stream or river. If the bottom is rough and rocky and you have to search among large boulders, the smaller

The author has located a metallic-reading object with his VLF type detector. The object can be a gold nugget, a spent bullet, or some metallic article lost by an early-day miner. All of the material he scoops out will be panned as panning is one sure way to retrieve even the smallest of gold nuggets that may have caused the detector to respond. It is more difficult to search for black sand deposits in an area like this because often many of the large rocks are themselves mineralized, and they produce detector signals the same as black magnetic sand. Both the BFO and VLF type detectors can be used for locating nuggets in black sand deposits.

(5″ to 8″) searchcoil will be more practical. If the bottom area is smooth and sandy and you wish to get all the depth possible, then choose the 8″ to 12″ to obtain both reasonable ease in maneuvering and maximum depth. An absolutely *drift free* detector is a must in the cold mountain streams. The water temperature was one of the major stumbling blocks encountered in previous search attempts in such areas before the invention of zero-drift circuits and searchcoils.

Set the tuning at the manufacturer's recommended setting. This will enable you to distinguish the response more clearly. If you are using the smaller searchcoils, 5″ or 8″, it would be to your advantage to tune in the metal mode. As you pass over the concentrations of black magnetic sand, the sound will decrease; but, should you pass over a large-size metallic GOLD nugget, the sound would increase. With practice you would still be able to distinguish the black sand pocket while having the opportunity perhaps to locate an unusually large gold nugget or metal object.

When using the larger BFO searchcoils, 8″ or 12″, tune in the mineral mode of operation. The coil size is such that the detection of small metallic objects (like gold nuggets) would be almost impossible. Tuned in the mineral mode the beat would increase as you pass the mineralized pocket of black sand, thus giving you better ground coverage and more depth with the larger coils.

Fred Heine and Jack Dean, owners of this recently-developed lightweight 4" gold dredge, are attempting to locate black sand concentrations with a Garrett BFO Master Hunter. Mrs. Jack Dean and Vi Sansom are assisting with the dredge. Notice the newly-designed system of water discharge into the twin 15" sluice boxes. Information on purchase of or dealerships for dredging equipment may be obtained by writing OREGON GOLD DREDGE, LTD., Eugene, Oregon 97402 or calling (503) 343-6741.

If two or more operators are using a metal/mineral detector in conjunction with the underwater suction dredge, it is sometimes possible to choose the more heavily concentrated areas for dredging. One person can operate the detector and the other, the dredge. Your success will depend on the condition of the stream bed and whether it is possible to operate in and among all the boulders.

For dry land searches utilize the same methods as described above. Coil size will govern whether you might discover an unusually large nugget while conducting the black sand search. Also, the correctly tuned detector will give true readings on either black sand pockets or on conductive metallic objects. Testing of various types of detectors will quickly confirm the VLF/TR or BFO to be the most practical choice for this type of prospecting.

GOLD PANNING MADE EASY!

During the gold rush days of the late 1800's and early 1900's gold panning was back-breaking labor, and unless the early-day panners hit a lucky spot panning was not very profitable. Today, gold panning is a lot easier and more profitable in terms of gold recovered for the amount of work performed. This is due not only to the greatly increased price of gold but also to the new, efficient "Gravity Trap" Gold Pan.

The "Gravity Trap" Gold Pan was designed by Roy Lagal of Lewiston, Idaho, and is manufactured and distributed by Garrett Electronics. Made of light but durable ABS plastic, the pan weighs much less than the old style metal pans. More importantly, the "Gravity Trap" Pan has built-in gold traps in the form of 90-degree riffles. These riffles trap the heavier gold and allow fast "panning off" of the unwanted rocks and gravels. Using this new pan a weekend or recreational placer miner can work with much greater efficiency than the most proficient professional using the old style metal pan.

By using a metal/mineral detector to locate black sand deposits and then panning the promising locations with a "Gravity Trap" Gold Pan, today's recreational miner can produce good results. Not everyone who hunts gold can get rich. It is safe to say that weekenders and vacationers, if they pursue placer (pronounced *plas-er*) mining properly, can offset some of their expenses by panning gold. Even more satisfying than the recovery of gold is the pleasure of sitting by a clear water mountain stream or a long-forgotten dry gulch, producing income by working with your hands.

With this new pan even dry stream beds can produce gold. This pan allows both wet and dry panning since the built-in riffle design can be depended upon to trap the gold. In fact, the dry streams which have not seen water for many years can be very productive as they probably were passed by during the busier gold rush days. The old-timers with their less efficient metal pans preferred to pan with running water because the work was easier. With today's modern metal detector and the efficient "Gravity Trap" Gold Pan, new gold-producing areas are being discovered daily, and the known producing areas of the past are yielding gold that the old-timers missed. The fun, excitement, and profit of recreational mining are waiting out there in the beautiful gold country, and the treasure hunters of today are limited only by their time and desire.

HIGH PRICED GOLD HELPS CREATE NEW WORLD GOLD RUSH!

While people have known about the vast quantity of detectable and recoverable gold that remains in the gold fields of the world, a sudden jump in the world market value of gold and several large finds were the sparks that set off today's new electronic gold rush. A 56-ounce gold nugget was recently found in a gold region in Southern California. In northern California where large gold nuggets were found during the 19th-century gold rush, prospectors searching with VLF/TR metal detectors report finding large nuggets missed by early-day miners because, unlike electronic equipment, they could not see into the ground.

In the states of Washington, Oregon, Idaho, Montana, among others, and in Canada, metal detectors are being put to use at a pace never before equaled. Nuggets and veins of gold, as well as silver, are being found, veins that otherwise might never have been discovered. Throughout various countries, prospectors are finding gold with gold pans and dredges. When the price of gold was low, it was not worthwhile to recover gold in this manner. Now, however, weekend hobbyists and vacationers are finding that their gold panning efforts are paying off.

Members of The International Treasure Hunting Society have made several trips into the fabled silver mining districts of Mexico's Sierra Madres mountain range. Using electronic devices, these prospectors have surveyed old, worked out mines and have detected several large and rich veins of pure native silver. Veins of silver that lay within inches of the mine walls, ceilings, and floors responded to the seeing-eye capabilities of the VLF/TR. Veins that were walked over or passed by for decades were finally brought to light by these hunters who had the spirit of adventure and faith in their skills and equipment.

Recently, in Australia, gold nuggets as large as your head have been found with the new VLF/TR instruments. Nuggets ranging in size from one pennyweight to several ounces are being

GOLD PANNING IS EASY!

"WET" PANNING in streams for gold, silver, mercury, platinum, garnets, sapphires, rubies, and other gem stones.

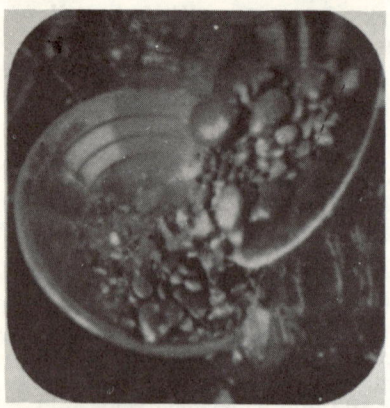

#1 Beginners who have never "panned" gold can gain confidence and skill by placing a few birdshot (BB's) in pan with gravel, dirt, or sand, and practicing "panning" in any large water container (such as a wash tub).

#2 Place selected gravel, sand, etc., in pan. Place pan UNDER water. Use hands to break up or dissolve clay or mud balls and remove larger rocks. Let small gravel or sand sift through fingers back into pan. CAUTION: *keep pan under water at all times.*

#3 Keeping pan under water, rotate pan with swirling motion, causing the gravel and sand to "loosen", thus letting the heavier gold or precious metals/minerals settle to the bottom. Tilt forward edge of pan slightly "down" while letting dirty water, light sand and gravel gradually wash over the edge of pan.

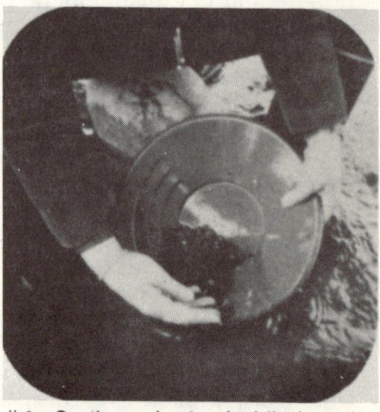

#4 Continue circular (swirling) motion, pausing occasionally to rake the "top" or "cleaned" material back into the water. CAUTION: *keep pan under water at all times.* BB's, GOLD, or any material of HIGH SPECIFIC GRAVITY will begin settling to the bottom of the pan. The SHARP 90° riffle traps will do the rest.

#5 Eventually you will have only a small amount of heavy concentrated material left in the pan riffle traps. Start using a gentle, but firm, side-to-side motion and let lighter material on top gradually slip over edge of pan. You may use either one hand or both for this side-to-side motion, but keep all material being separated UNDER WATER.

#6 Tilt the forward edge of pan "upward" or back toward you occasionally. This causes the heavier concentrates to "gather" or become trapped in the built-in GRAVITY TRAP and eliminates chances of losing light GOLD (BB's, etc.) Continue side-to-side motion, occasionally raising the pan from water, letting the lighter material wash off.

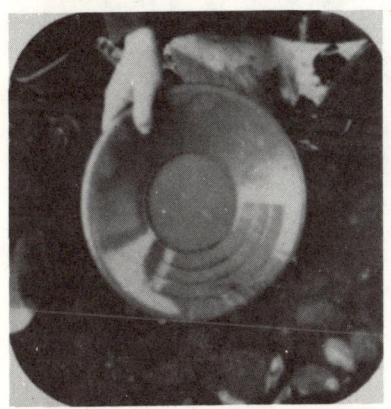

#7 The heaviest concentrates are now caught in the "Gravity Traps". Continue side-to-side motion (under water), and slowly raise the back side of pan, letting the lightest material slip over the edge. STOP when you are down to approximately ONE teaspoon full of material. Dip small amount of water into pan and carefully spread the concentrates.

#8 Carefully inspect the remaining black sand for nuggets, tiny specks of GOLD, GARNETS, SAPPHIRES, or other precious metals/minerals. (Your practice BB's will be there.) The "Gravity Trap" gold pan has done its job — QUICKLY, PROFESSIONALLY and PROFITABLY. Show your friends how *easy* it is with the new "Gravity Trap" gold pan. Remember the list of RAM books that show WHERE and HOW to find *Gold* and minerals.

found every day in the old, early-day mining districts. One-ounce to twenty-ounce nuggets are very common, and nuggets weighing twenty-five to fifty-ounces are reported regularly. The largest nugget found to date exceeded 200-ounces troy! It is no wonder that newspapers the world over are printing stories about these remarkable finds. With gold and silver prices much higher than most people ever thought they would be and with new advances in metal detectors and prospecting equipment, it seems likely that this new rush for Mother Earth's precious metals will continue for a long time. Those who sharpen their detecting and prospecting skills and go in search of the treasures of the earth stand a good chance of being greatly rewarded!

Editor's Note: The two best books to study and learn from are THE COMPLETE VLF-TR METAL DETECTOR HANDBOOK and ELECTRONIC PROSPECTING. These books, coauthored by Roy Lagal and Charles Garrett, are the knowledgeable word written by the two top authorities on electronic prospecting and treasure hunting with today's advanced metal detection equipment. Both books, from Ram Publishing Company, may be obtained from your treasure hunting supplier or directly from Ram. See listing at end of book.

Here are a few more relics that Gene Rolls has added to his tremendous collection of treasure found in California ghost towns. Watchfobs, pendants, tokens, and commemorative pieces bring high prices on today's market. There are countless ghost towns where thousands of relics like Gene's can be found. There are many treasure hunters who specialize in searching ghost towns and they do quite well. Pick up a ghost town map of your state and head out! Most ghost towns are virtually untouched! Photo by Ray D. Rolls.

CHAPTER X

Searching for Battlefield Relics

The War Between the States, (1861-1865), a conflict between the American Union and the eleven Southern states which seceded to form the Confederate States of America, was a climactic event of nineteenth-century America. When measured by numbers engaged and casualties in proportion to population, it was the biggest of American wars and the biggest war anywhere in the century from 1815 to 1914.

Today many thousands of people have found an interesting pastime in the collecting and studying of artifacts and other items from the great home war. The values placed on most of the items reflecting the States War are often astronomical. Simple buttons from Union and Confederate uniforms have been sold at open and private auctions for as much as $1,000. Buckles, a favorite item with most collectors, are highly sought and often demand prices beginning as low as $10 for common buckles to more than $2,000 for the more rare or ornate buckles.

The numerous battle and skirmish sites of the Eastern and Western campaigns and naval operations abound in relics and artifacts valued by the States War buff and professional collector. All types of weapons or instruments of the War are being located today by the persistent metal detector operator. There are many "known" battle areas in the country now protected by State and Federal governments. These areas, rightfully so, are protected.

However, over 4,000 recorded battles were fought, and debris from these battles and unrecorded skirmishes and engagements can still be located in many parts of our country. With the proper research, a States War student or collector can find areas that have never been touched. A quality-built and dependable metal detector is absolutely essential to the battlefield searcher. There are numerous items buried from just below the ground's surface to several feet deep. Obviously, without the aid of the metal detector these valuable relics and artifacts would be missed.

Battlegrounds are numerous in the mid-Southern states. Most of these forgotten sites are located on private land, and it always pays dividends to seek and secure owner permission *before* conducting your search. Always use common sense and courtesy when searching and digging on private property. Fill your holes, pick up your litter, and leave the area as clean or

Author testing one of the new Master Hunter VLF type ground compensating detectors near Cripple Creek, Colorado. The new VLF type detectors allow the operator to completely balance out the adverse effects of negative mineralized ground without reducing the detector sensitivity. Sensitivity is actually greatly enhanced because of this new circuit technique. The VLF detector has become extremely popular with the ghost town and battlefield relic searcher.

cleaner than you found it. This will aid in attaining a standing invitation by the owner to return.

    Vast trenches and battery lines were dug by both sides during the States War. Many of these areas will yield fortunes in collectibles. Often a hasty retreat was necessary and the valuable items left behind are eagerly sought by today's collector. Some of these scorched battlegrounds saw not only heavy bombardment but fierce hand-to-hand combat, as well. With a keen ear and sensitive detector, a person can sometimes find coins, watches, rings and other personal items lost by the soldiers in the scuffle. Bayonets, swords, sabres, pistols, rifles, binoculars, and brass insignia of all types can be found around and in the trenches and bunkers.

    Anyone interested in American history, battlefield weaponry, or general treasure hunting should make a point to visit the Stanley Frank museum in Natchez, Louisiana. Mr. and Mrs. Frank have been systematically searching the Louisiana battlefields for many years, and have amassed one of the finest and most complete collections of battlefield weaponry in the country. Practically every kind of weapon used in the War can be found in their museum, along with thousands of other valuables located during their metal detecting activities. The Franks are always happy to guide the beginner in the right direction in positive pursuit of War relics. In the Dallas, Texas, area the Garrett Electronics Museum is a favorite with many avid treasure hunters. The numerous items displayed will excite the average person to become a hard-core treasure hunter and detector enthusiast. Guns, knives, War relics, Indian artifacts, coins, bottles, and insulators are just a few of the kinds of interesting and valuable items on display. This museum is located in Garland, Texas (near Dallas), at 2814 National Drive.

Many of the relics of the War era will never be found: city expansions, highways, and residential areas have covered them. However, if you suspect that a building project is being developed in a battle or camp area, contact the developer and request permission to conduct a search. Normally, permission will be granted and you will have the freedom to dig for the precious relics.

For a sample of the value placed on States War items, check the following price list: buttons—average $10-$400; buckles—average $10-$2,000; binoculars and telescopes—$20-$60; sabres — $25-$1,000; bullets and molds — $35-$100; canteens — $10-$150; saddles — $100-$500; corps badges — $35-$150; flags — $400-$3,500; handguns — $100-$12,000; insignia — $3-$75; mess gear — $3-$50; pikes — $35-$300.

The above partial price list should prompt you to investigate battlefield relic collecting as a hobby. Artifacts from this period in American history, as well as articles from other periods, are going to continue to demand and receive a healthy price.

The super-depth ground canceling VLF/TR type detectors should be used in battlefield relic hunting. Unbelievable depths are achieved with these new detectors. Minie balls are being detected to depths of eighteen inches and small cannon balls to more than three feet! These accomplishments were unheard of in the days of the TR and BFO. Since the majority of the battlefield areas contain heavy concentrations of magnetic iron mineral, the ground canceling feature of these new detectors eliminates what was formerly a disheartening problem.

Frankie proves there is still treasure to be found. This Spanish silver bar is one among many that were recently found by treasure hunters. The modern metal detector has been the key to the recovery of the majority of treasure finds that have been made during the past few years. With the advent of the new, very low frequency type of detectors, treasure hunters are now able to search much more deeply, even in highly mineralized areas that once were thought to be unworkable.

CHAPTER XI

Lost Treasure on the Beach!

For hundreds of years people have flocked to the beaches in search of pleasure, fun, and respite from problems of everyday life. Most come to lie in the sun and splash in the surf. Another group has been coming to the beaches for entirely different reasons. They seek lost treasure: coins, rings, watches and other jewelry lost by the modern day sun bather. These treasure seekers are also searching for the gold and silver coins, ingots and artifacts which originally were part of the cargoes of many wrecked ships which have found their final resting places amid the shallow offshore coastal waters. The fortunes awaiting these treasure hunters and coin hunters is estimated in the millions of dollars.

Sun bathers and swimmers lose coins, rings, watches, medallions, and all kinds of jewelry in countless numbers. It is easy to understand why. Take rings, for instance. People go swimming, play in the water, or run and are active on the beach in hot sun. They perspire and slosh on greasy sun tan lotion. If they are wearing rings, the rings can slip off their fingers. As people swim and make strokes in the water, throw balls, or generally run and engage in horseplay with one another, rings slip off their fingers and fall to the ground to become quickly mashed into the sand by foot traffic. Usually when people lose rings on the beaches they have no idea when or where they lost them. The same is true for other jewelry ... necklaces, medallions, watches, and so on. Many people carry coins loose in bathing suit or beach jacket pockets. These coins can quite easily fall out and be lost.

WHERE TO SEARCH

On an open beach one place might be just about as good as another. Sunbathers and swimmers and those who just watch are active all the way from shallow water areas back up into the limits of the beach or park. It's best, if you can, to observe swimmers, sunbathers and on-lookers on a crowded day. From such observations you will be in a better position to find the "hot spots". Always search around concession stands, piers, lifeguard towers, drinking fountains and locations of this sort where people congregate.

On some beaches there are roped off areas designated for swimming. By all means, search these places first. It's a good idea to strike up a conversation with, perhaps, the lifeguard or the concession stand operators. It may be that the swimming areas of by-gone days were located elsewhere on the beach. You would certainly want to search those sites. Also, lifeguards may know where rings and valuables are reported to have been lost. Try working along the water's edge at both low and high tides. Both could be profitable. You will encounter much less trash near the water, but remember some very valuable coins and jewelry have been found back away from the beach in the heavy traffic areas.

The metal detector is the best means available for locating coins, artifacts and valuable treasure site clues. Many people are now utilizing their detectors and dredges to clean out swimming and recreational underwater sites. If you are fortunate enough to find one or more of these unworked locations your rewards should be great. It is estimated that more than one-half of the coins, rings, jewelry and other items lost at swimming areas and on beaches are lost in the water. Thus, persons using a detector along beaches should also search in the water, provided their instruments are equipped with submersible searchcoils. Generally, a detector operator with this type of instrument can search to a depth of two to three feet, if he has some type of special digging probe.

Treasure hunting on the beaches is fun and enjoyable ... and who knows what you may turn up next!

Editor's Note: An excellent, very informative and instructional article about beachcombing was printed in the quarterly of The International Treasure Hunting Society, THE INTERNATIONAL TREASURE HUNTER, Vol. 2, No. 1. T. R. Edds of Merritt Island, Florida, wrote the in-depth article, explaining how to be successful when searching for coins, rings, and other jewelry with metal detectors. Edds is also writing a book, soon to be published by Ram Publishing Company, about treasure hunting the beaches. In the book Edds generously explains the secrets of success he has learned during the many years he has searched the Florida beaches. This new book will, we predict, quickly become a best seller.

CHAPTER XII

It Is Easy To Understand Metal Detectors

The history of detectors began in the late 1920's. A man working with radio instrumentation noticed that a nearby metal water tank was interfering with the radio's "tuning." Following a hunch that small metallic objects could be detected using radio gear, he was successful in locating small closeby metallic objects. Thus, the metal detector was born. The first detectors were of the Transmitter-Receiver (TR) type. They were large and bulky, often requiring two men to carry them. As the years progressed, detectors became smaller and more efficient. The war years brought about improvements in the form of mine detectors. Following WW II, small, hand-held transmitter TR detectors (slightly larger than today's detectors) were produced for utility companies and treasure hunters. Detectors of various types have been produced continuously since then.

Detectors do work, despite the claims of some who say they do not. They work quite well, whether they are detecting metals and some minerals underground, relics in buildings or metal objects lost under water. In fact, they work so well they do everything for you except actually dig the object! They can indicate reasonably well the size and shape of the detected object. They can even tell you if the object is worth digging up!

There are three basic types of detectors being built today. They are, alphabetically, the Beat Frequency Oscillator (BFO), the Transmitter-Receiver (TR), and the Very Low Frequency (VLF). These three types have different operating characteristics. Each will do some jobs better and other jobs not so well as the other. No type is more complex or difficult to build than another. Of course, cheap, low cost instruments are easy to build. Quality-built detectors are difficult to build, and much engineering and testing are required in order to produce detectors that will do the job they were built to do and to continue doing it year after year. In this book you have already read much about these three types. Now, we will look more deeply into how these detectors work and which jobs each is best suited to do. Read on ... detectors are easy to understand. You'll see!

As discussed earlier, the TR detector was the first type used by the treasure hunter. TR's have been produced continuously since the early thirties, though there was a slowdown in their production during World War II. Following the War, several companies began producing various TR models. Basically, they were all about the same. Improvements came very slowly. Patents were granted on some models. During the 1950's various persons and companies began producing BFO models. BFO models came about because of existing TR patent restrictions and because the BFO (even the early-day models) could be used very well in the prospecting field and in general TH-ing. In the early 1960's other companies began mass-producing BFO models. It was probably at this time that the average person, the weekend hobbyist and vacationer, began to take an interest in detecting as a fun and rewarding thing to do. To meet increased demands more detector companies sprang up. About this time existing TR patents expired, thus paving the way for others to produce copies of these TR's. Production of both BFO's and TR's began in earnest, and increased greatly during the 1960's.

METAL DETECTOR ELECTROMAGNETIC SEARCHCOIL FIELD PATTERNS

Have you wondered how a metal detector's searchcoil magnetic field search patterns really look and work? I have reproduced (from page 43 of E. S. LeGaye's *Electronic Metal Detector Handbook)* a drawing which shows the electromagnetic field lines as they are generated and caused to flow around a BFO detector's searchcoil. (See accompanying illustration.) This side view allows you to see the field lines as they circle around the coil and how they are crowded together INSIDE and below the coil. I have drawn the dotted "U"-shaped pattern below the coil to outline the area in which this crowding takes place.

You can see that the magnetic fields flow **around** the coil. In the center of the coil where we have drawn the dotted lines, the magnetic field lines become highly concentrated. Outside the coil, the magnetic field lines are less crowded. When a detector's electromagnetic field passes through metal, the electronic oscillators change frequency. It is this change in frequency that alerts the operator to a detected metal target. The stronger the magnetic field, the stronger will be the detector's output signals.

Thus, you will note that since the magnetic field is stronger in the center of the coil than outside the coil, THE STRONGEST DETECTOR SIGNALS WILL BE PRODUCED WHEN A METAL TARGET MOVES DIRECTLY UNDER THE COIL. Metal targets can be detected which are not directly under the coil, but the signals are much weaker. Fortunately, these stronger resulting signals allow us to "zero-in" on our detected object, thus saving much needless digging. If the detector's signals were the same regardless of where the target was located within the magnetic field, then we would be faced with an almost impossible task of pinpointing the detected object.

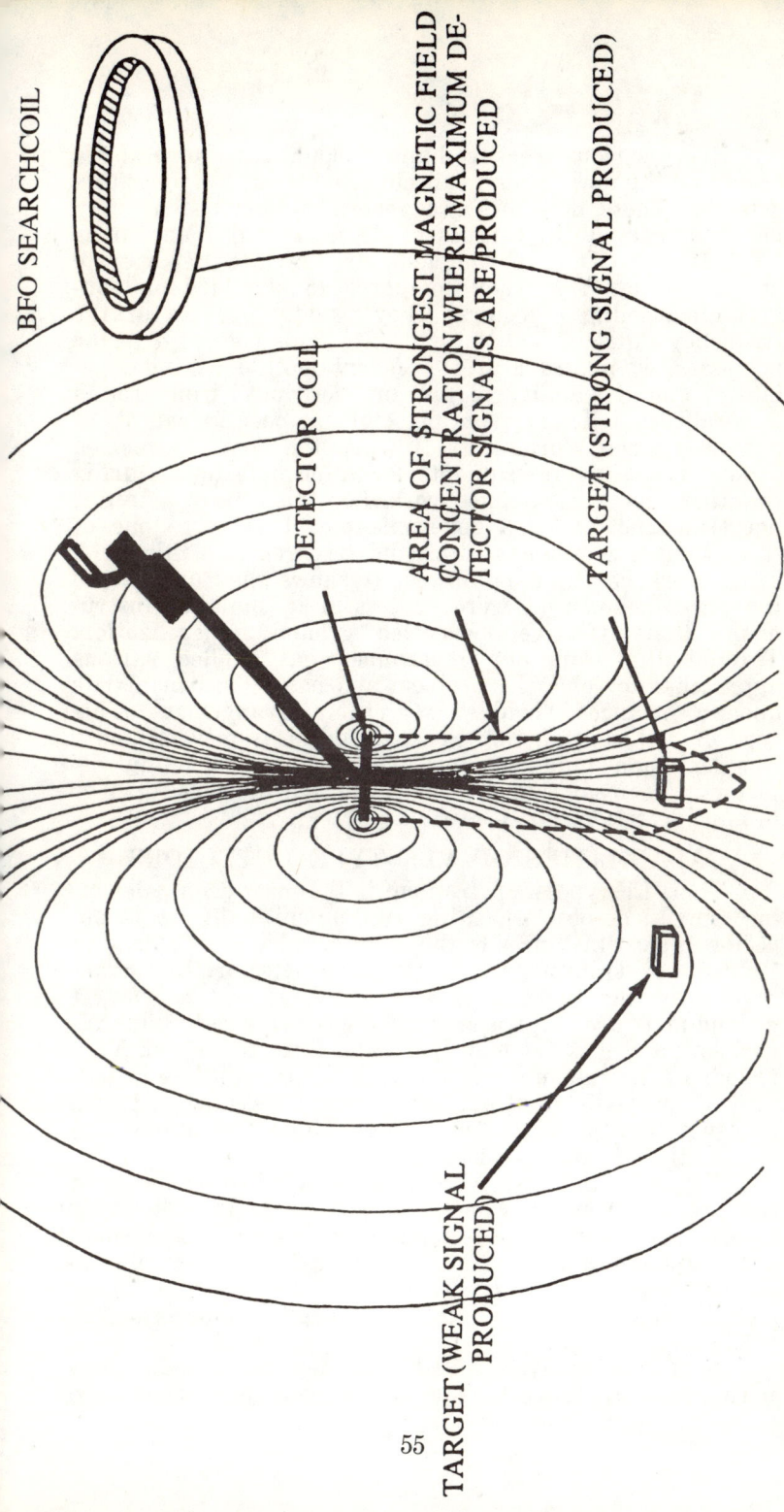

This illustration represents the electromagnetic field lines and resultant detection pattern produced by a BFO searchcoil. (See BFO discussion, this chapter.)

Every serious treasure hunter should soon have at his command the new ground canceling, mineral-free operation detector. These detectors are generally described as very low frequency (VLF) types of detectors (also known as GEB, MFO, GCD, GNC, magnum, *etc.*) because they operate at such a low frequency compared to standard or non-ground-canceling detectors. They usually operate in the frequency range of 500 Hz to 20 kHz. This type of detector possesses two main features: excellent depth-detecting capabilities and the ability to null or "zero out" iron ground mineralization. This type of detector has been known about and used since World War II when the Army developed ground canceling instruments for mine detection. During that time several companies worked on this type of detector, but Hazeltine, under a government contract, was one of the principal companies which did research into this field. Their work has been published. It shows they understood the phenomenon and were successful in building instruments that effectively canceled ground mineralization. Through the years our government has studied various approaches to solve the problem and has settled primarily upon a balanced "bridge" searchcoil arrangement. This type of coil construction arrangement is somewhat more complex than today's commercial ground canceling detectors. Not to say they are any better, but they are superior in mine detection.

CAPABILITIES OF VLF TYPE DETECTORS

The VLF type of instrument is the most deeply detecting, small-iron-object-locating instrument built. It is superior in most instances to the large-metallic-object-locating RF two-box transmitter-receiver type detector. Its advantages over the two-box type are that it will not detect ground moisture and water; it is not responsive to mineralized soil; and it is far more portable. Even though all VLF brands of instruments have remarkable capabilities in battlefield and relic hunting, prospecting, treasure and coin hunting, they do have limitations. These limitations and capabilities are discussed briefly below.

You will find your VLF type detector to be the most sensitive instrument you have ever used. It will easily detect small metallic objects, like square nails and small coins, to a depth of one foot and silver-dollar-sized coins to at least eighteen inches. Fruit jar lids, pots and larger metallic objects can be detected to depths of several feet with ease.

NOTE: Actually, the VLF type detector *is* a discriminating detector. When the operator adjusts the Ground Zero

"Hardrock" Hendricks, well-known treasure hunter and prospector, investigates a tree marking in his search for lost caches. In searches of this type "Hardrock" uses both the BFO type detector, pictured above, and the new VLF type ground-canceling deep-seeking detectors.

Control to "zero out" ground minerals, he has actually adjusted the detector to discriminate against or reject the ground minerals.

At this writing, no VLF's discriminate perfectly. VLF's with specially wound, full scan, co-planar coils discriminate by giving a signal over the full coil width when detecting iron but produce a signal over a narrow portion of the coil when detecting coins. This method allows up to about 85% accurate discrimination. Other VLF's discriminate by "whipping" the coil. To scan at normal speeds causes some or all of the signal to be lost.

As more and more of the VLF types are being used by coin hunters, however, the superiority of these new types is becoming obvious. Older and often more rare coins are being found in parks and other coin hunting areas where BFO and TR detectors have been used countless times. The VLF types are reaching down to almost unbelievable depths to detect even the smallest of coins. Obviously, when there is this type of success VLF type detector users begin to improve their skills with these detectors. They learn to "read" targets and leave much of the junk in the ground. For instance, small iron objects like nails produce "double" speaker blips when the searchcoil is passed over them in a certain direction. Let's say a small nail lies flat in the ground. The searchcoil is passed over the nail scanning from nine o'clock to three o'clock. A single blip is heard. When the searchcoil is passed over the nail scanning from six o'clock to twelve o'clock, a double blip is heard. This tells the operator that a small elongated iron object, such as a nail, is detected.

Some operators have become so skilled that they can, by careful scanning over detected objects from several directions, tell whether the object is round. In other words, they can fairly accurately determine if the object is a coin before they dig. There are other methods that VLF type detector operators have learned to use when they encounter a good coin hunting area that is trash littered. When the rewards are high, these operators learn to live with detector inadequacies.

The most popular VLF type utilizes two circuits: a VLF ground canceling circuit and a TR discriminator circuit. The operator can select one or the other circuit by flipping a switch. The ground canceling circuit is normally used, and when target identification is desired, the operator flips to the TR discriminator circuit and takes a quick "reading." The second design features a VLF and a TR discriminate circuit that operate simultaneously. These simultaneously operating circuits are designed primarily for coin hunting.

Their treasure hunting, prospecting, nugget hunting, and metal/mineral identifying capabilities are severly restricted. They do not provide true, VLF operation and fully adjustable TR discrimination modes. They are further limited because they use one coil size only and cannot be used with the larger, deep seeking, treasure hunting searchcoils. Also, they do a very poor job of rejecting bottlecaps and small pieces of flat iron targets which abound near parks, homesites, and other populated areas.

Regardless of manufacturer or detector classifications, all VLF detectors can be expected to produce better depth in the ground canceling mode than will the standard TR and BFO when used over highly mineralized ground. If shallow discrimination is achieved, it is the failure of the operator, not the detector. Any detector is only as good as the operator's skill. In the simultaneously operating circuit mode types, some unusual method of operating, such as "whipping" the searchcoil or operating complicated controls, is necessary. Unless the searchcoils are whipped rapidly, discrimination depth is decreased.

CACHE HUNTING

In any mineralized ground area where you are convinced that an extra-deep cache is located you should employ a VLF type detector. Even though this type detector responds to small pieces of trash buried very deeply, it is the most deeply seeking type detector for cache hunting. As stated earlier, it has advantages over the two-box transmitter-receiver in that it will not respond to water, moisture, slight changes in the earth's structure, and it is not responsive to mineralized ground. For cache hunting the VLF should be used with *large* searchcoils. Not only do you then get the benefit of the deepest possible penetration on larger-sized objects, but the larger the coil you use the less you will be bothered by small pieces of metal. Thus, the problem of digging deep holes for small junk metallic pieces is lessened.

VARIOUS SEARCHCOILS FOR VLF TYPE DETECTORS

Actually, all VLF type detectors, including other mineral-free operation, ground canceling detectors, are TR type detectors. They transmit and receive the same as TR type detectors. The difference is, basically, that VLF types operate at a much lower frequency. With more or less ability they "cancel "the earth's iron mineralization. Since they are transmitter-receiver type detectors, they must have one or more coils that transmit a signal and one or more coils

Charlie Weaver and Roy Lagal of Lewiston, Idaho, warm up by searching in this Nez Perce Indian Reservation Park located near Winchester, Idaho.

that receive a signal. Let's discuss the different types of searchcoils.

CO-PLANAR TYPES

Co-planar type coils have the transmitter and receiver coils positioned so that they are lying in the same plane. There are, as shown in the accompanying drawings, several different configurations of the co-planar coils. The CO-PLANAR configurations generally have two transmitter coils (T) with one receiver coil (R). When the detector is tuned, the receiver coil "receives" EQUAL BUT OPPOSITE amounts of the transmitted field. Thus, the resulting audio signal is zero or slightly positive, and just a slight amount of sound comes from the detector speaker. When any metallic substance comes into the vicinity of the magnetic field, the fields are disturbed so that the receiver coil "receives" an UNEQUAL amount of the transmitted field. The result is an increase in audio tone.

One frequently employed configuration using the co-planar coil construction is the specially wound, full scan type. This type construction uses two transmitter coils and one receiver coil. If you will study this design and the old style, narrow scan TR design that has been used for many years (discussed under TR detectors) you will see similarities in the way the coils are positioned. You will note the search pattern is somewhat "lumpy." This type of coil is good for VLF design, and it gives an excellent response

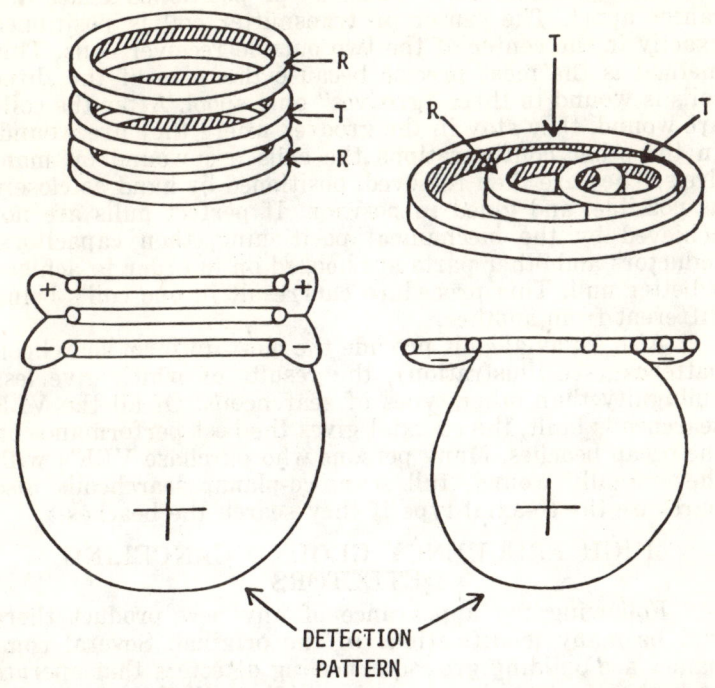

CO-AXIAL, STACKED LOOP
VLF TYPE SEARCHCOIL

4B CO-PLANAR
VLF TYPE SEARCHCOIL

The co-axial stacked loop VLF type searchcoil is shown on the left. It has one transmitter coil (T) sandwiched between two receiver coils (R). You will note that its detection pattern covers the full width of the searchcoil. The negative searchcoil areas, as shown to the left and to the right of the upper part of the positive pattern, are very small and lie outside the searchcoil diameter. The multi-wound, full scan, co-planar type searchcoil has three windings: two transmitter and one receiver coil. The detection pattern is only slightly more narrow than the co-axial type. These multi-wound, full scan co-planar type searchcoils have slightly less 60-cycle power line rejection than do the co-axial types.

characteristic that allows good rejection of iron targets and 60-cycle power line pickup.

CO-AXIAL TYPES

This type coil construction is very good because of its perfectly uniform and predictable response, plus the extreme accuracy with which it can be constructed. As seen in the illustration, the center, or transmitter, coil is positioned exactly and precisely so that all the coils are exactly the same diameter and "stacked" or positioned exact distances apart. The center or transmitter coil is positioned exactly in the center of the two outside receiver coils. This method is the most precise because the wire of the three coils is wound in three "grooves" on a spool. After the coils are wound, they stay in the grooves where they are wound. In the other configurations the coils are wound on mandrels. They are then removed, positioned by hand as closely as possible, and glued in position. If perfect nulls are not achieved by the mechanical positioning, then capacitors, inductors and other parts are hooked on in order to achieve a better null. This procedure can result in one coil's being different from another.

Also, co-axial coils provide the most uniform searchcoil patterns (see illustration), the results of which give less ambiguity than other types of searchcoils. Of all the VLF searchcoils built, the co-axial gives the best performance on the ocean beaches. Many persons who purchase VLF's with the specially wound, full scan, co-planar searchcoils also purchase the co-axial type if they search the beaches.

HIGH FREQUENCY GROUND CANCELING DETECTORS

Following the appearance of any new product there will be many modifications of the original. Several companies are building ground canceling detectors that operate at higher frequencies than the original VLF type ground canceling detectors. These higher frequency detectors can be called ground canceling detectors since they do an excellent job, but they do not possess the extreme depth capability of the VLF types. These higher frequency ground canceling detectors operate at frequencies up to 20 kHz (kilohertz) per second. This 20 kHz upper limit has been established rather arbitrarily since ground canceling detectors can be made to operate at frequencies as high as 100 kHz and higher. The higher the frequency, however, the less the sensitivity, especially when it comes to buried targets.

THE NEW VLF/TR GROUND CANCELING TYPES

To take advantage of both the excellent depth characteristics of the lower frequency VLF circuitry and the all-around capability of the higher frequency VLF circuitry, Garrett Electronics is manufacturing two distinct series of VLF/TR's. Both feature a VLF ground canceling (mineral free) circuit and a TR discriminating circuit. One series is the Master Hunter VLF/TR DEEPSEEKING series. The second series is the Master Hunter VLF/TR

FEATHERWEIGHT series, perhaps better known as the "GROUNDHOG" series.

THE MASTER HUNTER VLF/TR DEEPSEEKING SERIES

This series operates at 5.5 kHz. This lower frequency circuit produces extreme depth. Typically, a Civil War Minie ball and large coins can be detected deeper than two feet, even in highly mineralized ground. A quart size container can easily be detected three-and-one-half to four feet when the large, 14-inch searchcoil is used. This instrument features two circuits, a VLF ground canceling circuit and a TR discriminating circuit. The TR circuit operates much like a standard TR detector, except in highly mineralized ground a much more erratic response is noted. This deepseeker series offers an excellent degree of discrimination in the VLF mode, particularly when the specially wound, full scan, co-planar coils are used.

The Deepseeking series should be used only by those who are professional cache and coin hunters or by those who don't mind digging a lot of DEEP holes. Many operators prefer this type, however, because they can detect coins and other objects more deeply than with any other type of detector. They operate in the VLF mode and when they want to discriminate, they flip to the TR mode for a quick reading.

THE MASTER HUNTER VLF/TR FEATHERWEIGHT SERIES

This "Groundhog" series operates at 15 kHz. This higher frequency produces slightly less depth detection than the Deepseeker series, but superior, general purpose, all-around type detection results. Eighteen inches can be obtained on Minie balls or large coins. Quart containers can be easily detected from three to three-and-one-half feet when the large 10½-inch specially wound, full scan, co-planar searchcoil is used. The "Groundhog" also features two circuits, a VLF ground canceling circuit and a TR discriminating circuit.

The VLF/TR "Groundhog" offers superior operation in more modes than does any other type detector. Its VLF mode permits perfect operation over mineralized ground. Its specially wound, full scan, co-planar searchcoils give nearly perfect discrimination against iron while in the VLF mode. With the click of a switch, the TR discriminating mode is activated. While in this mode, a unique TR adjustment control is activated. It lets the operator select maximum depth detection of precious metal, iron caches (money in an iron pot), relics, coins, and jewelry.

If, for instance, maximum depth detection of relics or caches (money in an iron pot) is desired, the TR Selector control is rotated to the 9 o'clock position. If the ground is littered with nails and other small iron objects, the control should be rotated to the 12 o'clock position. The small, bothersome iron targets will not be detected; only larger iron objects will be detected. A small amount (approximately 5%) of sensitivity to iron is lost in this 12 o'clock position. To detect coins to maximum depth, the control should be rotated to the 2 o'clock position. If the ground is littered with bottlecaps, they can be rejected by rotating the control to a position between 3 and 4 o'clock. Aluminum pulltabs and screw caps can also be rejected by rotating the control slightly further. Rotation clockwise from the "Maximum Coins" position (2 o'clock) reduces non-ferrous metal sensitivity slightly.

The new VLF/TR "Groundhog" series has rapidly become a favorite of the coin hunter. In both the VLF and TR modes, depth detection is much greater than that of standard TR's. Great depths have been reported, such as a nickel at 11 inches and a silver dollar at 14 inches. Even these depths are not the limit, however. Many people have reported that they are finding many valuable and deep coins in parks that have been worked "clean" with all other types of detectors.

FULLY ADJUSTABLE DISCRIMINATION CONTROLS

Fully adjustable discrimination controls are continuous adjustment controls (no discrete, fixed step settings) that allow minute adjustments so necessary to achieve exacting acceptance and rejection of conductive targets. When fully adjustable discrimination controls are used on the new VLF types that have correctly designed searchcoils, full treasure hunting capabilities are possible. Until now, only BFO detectors were classified as "all purpose" instruments. However, now that several new electronic improvements have been added to these new, all purpose, super-depth VLF's exciting new applications, never before thought possible, are suddenly available.

VLF TYPE DISCRIMINATING CIRCUITS

There have been many attempts to build VLF detectors with discriminating circuits that operate at the same time as the ground canceling circuits. "Whipping," adjustment of complicated controls and other attempts have achieved only varying degrees of success.

Most of the VLF types have a switch or selector control whereby the operator can use *either* the ground canceling mode *or* the TR discriminating mode. This dual circuit capability gives the operator more flexibility. Discriminating circuits that are installed on these VLF types work very well as far as discrimination goes. They can be adjusted to operate all the way through pulltab rejection while generally not losing as much sensitivity as do the standard TR discriminating detectors. Some VLF type discrimators lose only about five to ten percent sensitivity when adjusted for pulltab rejection.

Since the gain (electronic) of the VLF types is so very much higher than standard TR circuit gain, VLF types cannot be operated as easily over mineralized ground as can the standard TR's. For this reason, the VLF types have a gain or sensitivity control which permits the operator to reduce circuit gain to suit the conditions.

A problem one must live with is the extra weight of the VLF type searchcoils. Obviously, the heavier the weight of any searchcoil, the more physically demanding will be the operation of the detector over long periods of time. There are, however, arm rests available for use with some instruments which practically eliminate the extra fatigue associated with these detectors.

VLF/TR MULTI-WOUND, FULL SCAN, CO-PLANAR SEARCHCOIL DISCRIMINATION

One of the complaints about the VLF's was that discrimination was not available in the VLF mode. This problem has been mostly solved, with Garrett's multi-wound, full scan, co-planar searchcoils. In both VLF/TR Deepseeker and "Groundhog" series, searchcoil operation permits nearly perfect rejection of iron objects. It takes a few minutes' practice, but it is easy to learn to distinguish the signals. Iron gives a response over the full searchcoil width. Coins (and other precious metals) give a very narrow response at the exact center of the searchcoil. It soon becomes apparent that operation in the VLF mode with these new searchcoils gives the closest thing there is to "perfect" detector operation over mineralized ground.

MINERALIZED GROUND SEARCHING WITH PUSH-BUTTON VLF/TR DETECTORS

When ground minerals are present and ground canceling operation is desired, you can operate very efficiently using the following technique.

When an audio response is received, quickly criss-cross the target by making an "X" pattern to determine if the object is an elongated piece of magnetic ferrous iron. This is accomplished by listening for the double "blip-blip" response. If none is received, pass the searchcoil SLOWLY over the target to determine if the target response is WIDE or NARROW, indicating ferrous or non-ferrous. If you determine the target to be non-ferrous and deeply buried, OR if you are unable to identify it fully, place the searchcoil flat upon the ground over the target. Depress the push-button to retune the circuits. Slide the coil forward, backward, and then side-to-side to pinpoint the target exactly. Keeping your eye on the ground spot indicated by the "X" on the searchcoil, slide the coil to one side allowing the edge of the coil to clear the indicated target completely.

Keep the coil firmly on the ground and flip the mode switch to change operation from VLF (mineral-free) to TR discriminating mode. Depress the push-button to retune the circuit and slide the searchcoil gently back over the target. The TR discriminating circuit will identify the target as either good or bad, depending upon the rejection you have pre-set into the discrimination control.

The above-described searching procedure allows you to operate in the mineral-free mode, permitting the fastest

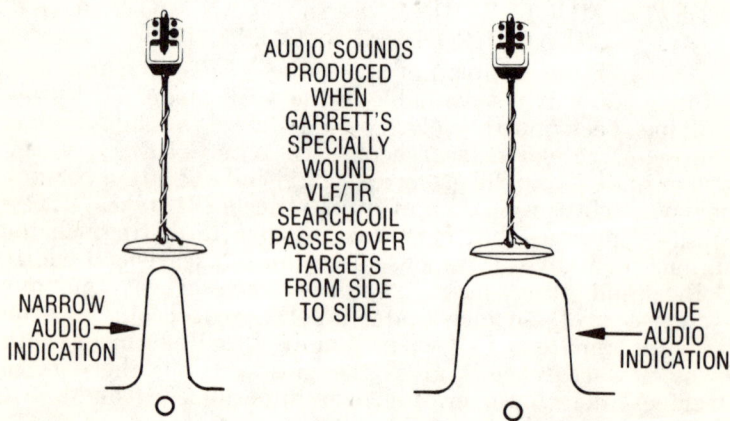

FRONT VIEW

AUDIO SOUNDS PRODUCED WHEN GARRETT'S SPECIALLY WOUND VLF/TR SEARCHCOIL PASSES OVER TARGETS FROM SIDE TO SIDE

NARROW AUDIO INDICATION

WIDE AUDIO INDICATION

Coins, non-ferrous, *etc.*, targets: Response begins at edge of searchcoil and peaks sharply at the center. Pinpointing is quick and highly accurate.

Bottlecaps, ferrous, *etc.*, targets: Response begins before edge of searchcoil is over target, thus producing easily identifiable response that is much wider than searchcoil width.

The above illustration shows how easy it is to discriminate when using the Garrett VLF/TR searchcoils. When iron objects are scanned over, a signal is produced over the full coil width. Non-ferrous objects, such as coins, gold bars, etc., produce a signal over a very narrow portion of the searchcoil. Only a few minutes' practice is required in order to achieve 75% to 85% accuracy.

ground coverage possible and producing the maximum depth necessary for fast, positive identification in the TR discriminating mode. This method is also used to identify correctly "out of place hot rocks" that are occasionally detected and identified as metal by VLF detectors.

SEARCH TRASH INFESTED AREAS SUCCESSFULLY

Those of you who have searched heavily laden trashy areas know how difficult it is to be accurate in pinpointing and identifying objects when other metal objects are close by. It is easy with push-button detectors.

When you have detected a target you want to pinpoint and/or identify, place the searchcoil on the ground directly above the target. Depress the push-button. (You should have the audio threshold set so that there is a faint speaker sound.) The instrument then tunes itself for that target and does not detect nearby targets when you slide the searchcoil back and forth over the main target.

This method can also be combined with sensitivity reduction when target litter is extremely bad. A highly sensitive detector that can be turned down has many advantages over a less sensitive detector that cannot be turned up!

MAKE AN HONEST EFFORT

To learn to utilize your discriminator more effectively, or any other detector, for that matter, make an honest effort to determine how your instrument reacts to all sorts of targets at various depths and over different types of mineralized ground. Little will be gained by burying objects and detecting them for practice. Newly buried objects cannot be detected as deeply as objects buried a year or longer. Also, close association of metals in the ground causes a different reaction.

It is best to analyze each target response you get. In other words, when you get an indication remember the strength of the signal; remember how wide a response you got on the surface of the ground; try to determine if it is a low growl or a high-pitched sound. Learn all you can about the signal, and then dig the object. As you retrieve the object note how deeply it is buried, the type of soil it was buried in, and how it was lying in the ground. Correlate this information with the signal response information you obtained when you first detected the object. If you do this with each object you dig up and try to understand what is occurring and why the signal reacted the way it did, you will greatly improve your ability to coin hunt successfully.

LEARN THE DIFFERENCES

So you see, there are definite operating differences and characteristics peculiar to each of the various types of detectors. All detector operators should fully understand the capabilities and characteristics of the two types of detectors. Recommended books are listed following Chapter XIV. They will explain the various types of detectors and their operating characteristics in much greater detail.

I strongly recommend that you continue your study of detectors. Without question, the most complete and advanced book about detectors is Roy Lagal's DETECTOR OWNER'S FIELD MANUAL, published by Ram Publishing Company. Roy has completely covered the field of metal detectors. He has fully explained all the different types and the jobs for which they are best suited. He explains *in detail* how to use each type of instrument in every possible application . . . something that has never been done before.

These guns, knives and relics are on display in the Garrett Electronics museum. All these relics were found by treasure hunters. The bent rifle in the upper left was found on a battle site where the Nez Perce Indians and the U.S. cavalry fought a battle in Northern Idaho. The slave chains on the right were found in Georgia. It is obvious that the chains saw much use because the links are badly worn. The fifth pistol from the top was found by a Marine on the beaches of Normandy during World War II. The pistol grip is painted bright red. Note the iron arrow points at left center. These were found by "Hardrock" Hendricks and Ed Bartholomew of Fort Davis, Texas. They are called trade arrows because the Spanish traded them to the Indians for hides, blankets, and other Indian goods.

Here is yet another glimpse into Roy Rolls' ghost town hunting success story. The coins speak for themselves! Photo by Ray D. Rolls.

CHAPTER XIII

Laws About Treasure Hunting

LET'S LEARN ABOUT TREASURE HUNTING LAWS

While I will not attempt to give legal advice, you need to become aware that there are laws applicable to various TH-ing situations. Each state has its own laws concerning where you can hunt for treasure and whether you may keep treasure when it is found. I will give you a few pointers on how to determine the laws of your locality.

All states have laws against trespassing. If a sign says, "Keep Out," do just that. It is always best to seek permission if it is possible to determine who owns the land. With the proper attitude and a true explanation of your purpose, you will be surprised at the cooperation you will receive from most landowners. The majority of them will be curious enough about your metal detector and what you hope to find to agree to let you search. Offer to split your find 50-50 and they will be even more willing. If large amounts of treasure are believed to be hidden or buried on another's property, a properly-drawn, binding legal agreement between both you and the landowner will eliminate any later disagreements which might otherwise arise.

In most cases, public property is open to you—parks, for example—if you do not destroy the grass or leave trash or holes. Most park superintendents know that conscientious treasure hunters pick up trash while coin hunting and leave the grounds in better shape than they found them. There are several ways to remove coins from the ground without digging a large hole or destroying the grass. My book, SUCCESSFUL COIN HUNTING, gives seven methods for retrieving coins properly. All treasure hunters must become aware of their responsibility to protect the property of others and to keep public property fit for all. Persons who destroy property, dig large holes and leave them unfilled or tear down buildings in search of valuables are not to be called treasure hunters but, more properly, looters or scavengers.

Learn of the laws in any area by calling the offices of the city and county attorneys and the chief of police. While some communities have laws against coin hunting in public parks, the police do not enforce the laws because past TH-ers have not caused damage but have, on the other hand, helped clean up the areas where they searched. However, in some cities the law may be strictly enforced so always check before searching.

When you make a significant find, the law may become more complicated. Treasure trover laws vary from state to state, and, accordingly, so do your rights to keep your find. Generally speaking, if the legal owner of the treasure can be proved the courts will usually award the treasure to that person, with a percentage of the trove awarded the finder. In some cases the state government may enter a claim.

UNCLE SAM'S INCOME TAX LAWS

Most income tax laws concerning treasure hunting are simple and easy to understand. Treasure hunting is a legal occupation and all income derived from treasure hunting is taxable as regular income. On the other hand, a definite advantage exists in your treasure hunting occupation because you are allowed to deduct necessary expenses. All expenses you incur while treasure hunting can be deducted. Meals, lodging, books, maps, tools and minor equipment are deductible in the year they are purchased. Major pieces of treasure hunting equipment, such as metal detectors and dredging equipment, are deductible over a three-year period. If your local Internal Revenue Service office tells you you cannot deduct your expenses, ask them if you have to declare the finds you make. If you must declare your finds, then by all rights you can deduct your expenses. If they ask you to deduct your expenses the year in which you declare your finds, THEN KEEP ACCURATE RECORDS!

All treasure you find must be declared as income during the year in which you receive monetary gain from that treasure. If you find $1,000.00 in coins that you spend because they have no numismatic value, then you must declare their face value in that year's income tax report. If, however, you find a valuable coin or, say, an antique pistol, you do not make a declaration until you sell the item and then only for the amount you received for it. If you decide to donate some of your finds to historical societies or museums, you may deduct the fair market price of the items as charitable contributions.

Simply stated, the tax laws require you to declare all income from treasure hunting. Therefore, all expenses necessary to gain that treasure hunting income are deductible. Think about it ... only professional guides are allowed to make deductions for their fishing equipment or hunting rifles! But you, as a hobbyist, can enjoy the same benefits.

CHAPTER XIV

Conclusion

As stated previously, treasure hunting is undoubtedly on the move as one of the nation's fastest-growing hobbies. The rewards are many, whether in a tangible form as the result of a good find or in just getting out, breathing fresh air and exploring our great American history.

Treasure hunting clubs and organizations are springing up all over the nation with a common goal of offering the amateur treasure hunter a collective source of information, procedures, marketing for his finds and sharing with his comrades the knowledge gained from the bounty discovered.

To be sure, there is considerable wealth awaiting the treasure hunter. This wealth can be found by diligent and persistent searching. After all, that is what treasure hunting is all about—to explore where other people have been and to discover the things they left behind!

I would be remiss in my promotion of treasure hunting as a great hobby if I did not remind you of some basic restrictions regarding private property, hunting without permission and property damage. The good name of treasure hunting and its enthusiasts must be protected or we will lose our rights to explore our own land. The following few paragraphs should be read and the ideas kept in mind if our hobby is to prosper.

If you wish to detect on private property always secure permission from the property owner first. Occasionally, by properly identifying yourself and your equipment, you will be able to gain permission to search an area which normally would be restricted to you. You may be allowed to search where others have not. You may discover that the property owner will be willing to assist you. You and the property owner should work out a mutually beneficial arrangement for distribution of all finds. Certainly always have respect for the property of others. Never leave holes or in any way mar the grounds. If even one treasure hunter does damage, regardless of how slight, the next treasure hunter may be denied permission to search. YOU might be that NEXT treasure hunter, or you may want to RETURN to an area!

If you wish to search a schoolground, seek permission from the Principal. Permission to search in city parks should be obtained from the office in charge of administering the park system. Before searching churchgrounds obtain permission from the person in charge at that church.

And, so... it is my desire that this brief glimpse of Treasure Hunting has given you an idea of what TH-ing is all about. Once you have become involved you will find many excellent sources of information to help you greatly develop your TH-ing interests. Begin to exercise your judgment now. Gather all the information you can and think out your treasure hunting plans and goals.

If you haven't already selected your metal detector, carefully analyze your interests and requirements in order to select one that will allow you to do everything you want to do. Learn which types of detectors perform best when used in the types of treasure hunting YOU are planning. Consider quality, performance and the manufacturer's reputation. After you have made your selection, put miles on that detector. Use it. Have fun with it. The rewards are great, and your only limitation is your available time.

As you meet other treasure hunters you will become aware of the almost fraternal relationship that exists among them. There are always stories to be swapped, recovered items to be displayed, and treasure hunting clubs to join. Learn as much as possible from more experienced treasure hunters. Learn their "tricks" and benefit from their knowledge. Many men give unselfishly of their know-how. Soon you will have your own knowledge to share with the newcomer. This fraternal aspect is one of the reasons why TH-ing has grown so greatly in such a short period of time. It is just like the proverbial snowball; it grows larger and gains momentum each year.

Do not neglect the tremendous knowledge that is available to you in the many excellent treasure hunting books. Walk with the professionals to learn their secrets. Start where they left off and write your own treasure hunting story!

If you have decided to join the ranks of TH-ers, "Welcome!" Within our ranks you'll find some of the most active, interesting and friendly people in the world. I personally know of no other hobby that has so few limitations. The sky is the limit, and there is no age barrier. If there is a more perfect outdoor hobby, I haven't found it!

One final "warning"... the treasure hunting bug is like a disease. Once it bites, there is no turning back, nor is there a vaccine to control it! It can make you a wealthy person, but, above all, it will improve your mental and physical health.

I WISH YOU A LIFETIME OF HAPPY AND SUCCESSFUL HUNTING!

Charles Garrett

Presented by
The International Treasure Hunting Society....

Thousands of treasure hunters took time out to attend the First International Competition Treasure Hunt which was held in the Dallas-Fort Worth, Texas, area. This hunt was sponsored by The International Treasure Hunting Society which is the first world-wide treasure hunting organization. More than $100,000 in prizes were won by these contestants as they searched the field with detectors of all kinds. Both young and old, professional and amateur took home many prizes. If you would like additional information on how to become a member of the ITHS and start receiving its publication, THE INTERNATIONAL TREASURE HUNTER, write to P. O. Box 3007, Garland, Texas 75041.

ARE YOU INTERESTED...

In treasure and coin hunting, relic collecting, ghost-towning, prospecting and/or nugget hunting? For free information on how to get outfitted properly and be successful in the great outdoor hobby of metal detecting visit your local equipment supplier. The new, correctly calibrated VLF/TR Ground Canceling Detectors are being used successfully all over the world. You can easily enter this profitable and exciting field.

ALABAMA: Birmingham, P & S Business Machines, 4511 5th Avenue So., 35222, (205-595-8322); **Flat Rock,** Walter B. Sloan, Rt. 2 Box 343, 35966 (205-632-2152); **Florence,** John G. Link, 310 Colonial Drive, P.O. Box 682, 35630, (205-766-0087); **Gadsden,** Owens Construction Co., 1806 Macarthur Street, 35901, (205-547-3049); **Huntsville,** Alabama Treasure Hunter, 909 Chatterson Road, 35802, (205-881-7772); **Lanett,** Belcher's Coins, 19 South 16th Street, 36863, (205-644-1881); **Mobile,** Confederate Ordnance, 2202 Government Street, P.O. Box 66075, 36606, (205-473-3731); **Oxford,** Hoff meyer's, 1429 Snow Street, 36203, (205-831-7730).

ALASKA: Homer, R & R Detectors, P.O. Box 1707, 99603, (907-235-8200); **Kodiak,** Nelson Enterprises, P.O. Box 814, 99615, (907-486-3672); **Wasilla,** Sluice Box, P.O. Box 382, 99687, (907-376-2365).

ARIZONA: Phoenix, Lucky Treasure World, 6005-D West Thomas, 85033, (602-247-4506); **Scottsdale,** The National Treasure Hunters League, 7350 East Jenan Drive, 85254, (602-948-0329); **Tempe,** The Treasure Shack, 2190 E. Apache, 85281, (602-968-0783); **Tucson,** Desert Trails, 230 West Ajo Way, 85713, (602-624-3804); Morey Detector Sales, 3825 E. Hardy Drive, 85716 (602-323-0071).

ARKANSAS: Camden, W. W. Mosley, P.O. Box 7, 768 Crestwood Rd., 71701, (501-836-5314); **El Dorado,** Herring Electric, 1217 West Hillsboro Street, 71730, (501-862-3928); **Harrison,** Ozark Treasure Hunter League, Industrial Park Rd., 72601, **Hazen,** Wil-Mar Detectors, Box 347, 72064 (501-255-3208 and 255-4493); **Little Rock,** Bill's Detectors, 5623 R Street, P.O. Box 7347, 72217, (501-666-6355); **Mountain Home,** Trammell's, 619 Baker Street, 72653, (501-425-3615); **Piggott,** Feather Lite Mfg., Co., P.O. Box 31, 227 East Jackson, 72454, (501-598-3669); **Pine Bluff,** Southeast Arkansas Gold and Silver Exchange, 1015 Cherry Street, 71601, (501-535-1090); **Rogers,** L. L. Lincoln, Route 1, 158 Pyramid Drive, 72756, (501-636-6867).

CALIFORNIA: Auburn, Lo Sierra Mining Equipment, 179 Palm Avenue, 95603, (916-823-1880); **Bakersfield,** C & J Detector Sales, 3104 Pepper Tree Lane, 93309, (805-397-0641); **Bellflower,** G.C. De Fabrizio & Assoc., 16238 Lakewood Blvd. 90706, (213-925-2271); **Bloomington,** Leonard Phye, 868 Ironwood Avenue, 92316, (714-823-6165); **Blythe,** Walter Graef, P.O. Box 169, 92226, (714-922-2579); **Brea,** Brea Bicycle & Sporting Goods, 141 S. Brea Blvd., 92621, (714-529-3353); **Buena Park,** Aurora Prospecting Supply, 6286 Beach Blvd., 90620, (714-521-6321); **Carmel,** Treasure Finders, 27383 Schulte Road, 93923, (408-375-1934); **Chowchilla,** Rencher Welding & Machine Works, 312 Calusa Avenue, 93610, (209-665-4219); **Colfax,** The Mine Shaft, Railroad & Oak Street, 95713, (916-346-2937), (24 Hr.); **El Dorado,** Thomas Murry, P.O. Box 406, 6001 Pleasant Valley Road, 95623, (916-622-5245); **Forest Ranch,** Roy Gene Rolls, Hwy. 32 at Sugar Pine, 95942, (916-342-4829); **Fresno,** Fresno Hobby & Crafts, 3026 N. Cedar, 93703, (209-226-4880); **Imperial Beach,** South Bay Coins and Stamps, 818 Palm Avenue, 92032, (714-423-2551); **Lafayette,** Fumble Fingers, 1027 Brown Avenue, 94549, (415-284-7406); **Lancaster,** Antelope Acres Market, Ron Farrell, 48011 90th St.

West, 93534, (805-948-4190, 942-7165); **Lodi,** Pay Dirt Mining Supply, 225 North California Street, 95240, (209-334-6565); **Modesto,** Gold Nugget Miner's Supply, 1302-9th Street, 95354, (209-529-5277); **N. Hollywood,** Treasure Emporium, 6507 Lankershim Blvd., 91606, (213-985-5217); **Northridge,** Keene Engineering, Inc. 9330 Corbin, 91324, (213-993-0411); **Orange,** Allied Services, 966 No. Main Street, 92667; **Pasadena,** Cal-Gold, 2400 East Foothill Blvd., 91107, (213-792-6161); **Riverside,** Pioneer Recoveries, 3510 Audubon Pl., 92501, (714-682-4302); **Rosemead,** Bill & Melba Dibble, 8851 E. Lansford Street, 91770, (213-287-7996); **Salinas,** B. C. Douglass, 1537 Placer Way, 93906, (408-449-1131); **San Bruno,** Dennis E. Witkowsky, Coins and Supplies, P.O. Box 772, 94066, (415-589-8179); **San Diego,** Gem & Treasure Hunting Enterprises, 2493 San Diego Avenue, 92110, (714-297-2672), (Closed Monday & Tuesday); **San Fernando (Lakeview Terrace),** Arts & Hobbies, 12323 Forest Trail, 91342, (213-899-1997); **San Francisco,** Mining & Lapidary, 131 10th Street, 94103, (415-626-6016); **Santa Maria,** Johnny's Metal Detectors, 207 N. Broadway, 93454, (805-922-8703); **Shandon,** Price's Treasures, P.O. Box 201, 93461, (805-238-6487); **Signal Hill,** Hidden Rod Shop, 2623 Gardenia Avenue, 90806, (213-427-8060); **Simi Valley,** Gemstone Equipment Mfg. Co., Inc., 480 E. East Street Bldg. 1, 93065, (805-527-6990).

COLORADO: Boulder, H. Glenn Carson Enterprises, 801 Juniper Avenue, 80302, (303-449-8079); **Colorado Springs,** Terry's Treasure Hut, 1217 N. Circle Drive, Circle East Shopping Mall, 80909, (303-597-4709); **Denver,** C & D Detection Enterprises, 5885 W. 38th Avenue, 80212, (303-424-7780); **Englewood,** The Prospectors Cache, 25 W. Girard, 80110, (303-781-8787); **Pueblo,** Lost Coin Treasure Instruments, 3921 Devonshire (Starlite Hills Shopping Center), 81005, (303-564-1061).

CONNECTICUT: Middletown, Beachcomber's Detector Sales, 2330 South Main Street, Ext., 06457, (203-347-2392); **Stratford,** Edward Perchaluk, 304 Circle Drive, 06497, (203-378-1660); **Suffield,** J & E Enterprises, 1242 South Street — Route 75, 06078, (203-668-0029).

FLORIDA: Fort Lauderdale, Josh Wilson's Detector Sales, 4704 NE 17th Avenue, 33334, (305-776-1076); Lawson Studio, 1503 East Las Olas Blvd., 33301, (305-463-5311); **Fort Walton Beach,** James R. Ford Treasure Chest, 528 N. Eglin Pky. 32548, (904-863-1595); **Hallandale,** Silver & Gold Metal Detectors, 24 N.W. First Street, 33009, (305-457-9999); **Jacksonville,** Old Kings Road Treasure Inn, 6946 Old Kings Road So., 32217, (904-733-1928); **Leesburg,** Palm Plaza Cards & Gifts, 713 N. 14th, 32748, (904-787-4661); **Maitland,** Kellyco Detector Distributors, 1443 S. Orlando Avenue, 32751, (305-645-1332); **Melbourne,** Zephyr Treasures, 2898 Zephyr Lane, 32935, (305-254-2796); **Merritt Island,** Mail Order Electronics, 200 Mustang Way 13-B, P.O. Box 1133, 32952, (305-452-8236); **Miami,** American International, 1850 NW 133rd Street, 33167, (305-821-1500); Seatech Metal Locators, 985 N.W. 95th Street, 33150, (305-693-1431); **Oakland Park,** Josh Wilson's Detector Sales, 4704 N.E. 17th Avenue, 33334, (305-776-1076); **Pensacola,** Redisco Inc. 12th Avenue Drugs, 2435 N. 12th Avenue, 32503, (904-433-6563); **Tampa,** Carl Anderson, Box 13441, 33611; **Tampa,** Florida Treasure Hunters, 907 23rd Avenue, 33605, (813-226-3824); **Tampa,** Treasure Shack, 3934 Britton Plaza, 33611, (813-833-9841).

GEORGIA: Atlanta, Southeastern Treasure Hunters, 985 Woodland Avenue S.E., 30316, (404-627-6019); **Decatur,** Finders Company, 225 Upland Road, 30030, (404-377-0974, Call Evenings); **East Point,** Ernest M. Andrews, Atlanta Tri-City Area, 2755 Sylvan Rd., 30344, (404-766-8141); **Mableton,** C.A.C. & Detector Sales, 6579 Factory Shoals Road (Near Six Flags), 30054, (404-948-1181); **Waycross,** J. C. Ballentine, P. O. Box 761, Hatcher Point Mall, 31501, (912-285-3250).

IDAHO: Coeur d'Alene, Sign Mart, 4905 Industrial Drive West, 83814, (208-772-3093); **Lewiston,** Tommie T. & Sue Long Outdoor Hobby Supply, 2416½ E. Main, 83501, (208-743-1768); **Pocatello,** Powers Candy Co., Powers Home Games & Hobbies, 602 S. 1st Avenue, 83201, (208-232-1693).

ILLINOIS: Bloomington, Rene's Treasure Trove, 214 East Front Street, 61701, (309-829-4538, 829-4058); **Chebanse,** Jerry's Treasure Hunter's Supply, RR #1, Meents Lane, 60922, (815-939-3815); **Galesburg,** Detectors Unlimited, 1671 Summit Street, 61401, (309-342-4032); **Lombard,** Electronic Exploration, 575 W. Harrison Rd., 60148, (312-620-0618); **Moline,** Hidden Treasure, Rev. John J. Costas, 3116 11th Avenue "A", 61265, (309-797-3098); **Pekin,** D & D Metal Detector Sales, 206 Reservoir Rd., 61554, (309-346-4377); **Quincy,** Mid-West Treasure Detectors, 507 So. 8th Street, 62301, (217-223-4723); **Waukegan,** Tom's Pool Center, Inc., 801 North Green Bay Rd., 60085, (312-244-4505); **Wedron,** Memory House, 1 N. Chestnut Street, 60557, (815-434-3568).

INDIANA: Anderson, Pat's Metal Detectors, RR. #7 Box 145, 46011, (317-378-0475); **Decatur,** O-D Western Store, Robert A. Everett, RR #5, 46733, (219-724-2097); **Fort Wayne,** A-Z Coins & Stamps, Glenbrook Center, 4201 Coldwater Rd., 46805, (219-483-3743); **Hammond,** J & J Coins, 7019 Calumet Avenue, 46324, (219-932-5818); **Indianapolis,** L & M Sales, 7310 Hazelwood Avenue, 46260, (317-255-4236); **Indianapolis,** The Prospectors Pouch, Indiana Treasure Hunting Headquarters, 246 S. Butler Avenue, 46219, (317-356-7343); **Oaklandon,** Pioneer Metal Detector, 10338 Pendleton Pike, 46236, (317-823-4202 or 898-4510); **Seymour,** Wray's Treasure Shop, RR #5, 47274, (812-497-2537).

IOWA: Baxter, Richard Cross, 314 South Main, 50028, (515-227-3391); **Bettendorf,** Ralph Barnett, 2918 Summit Hill Ct., 52722, (319-355-6366); **Cedar Rapids,** Cedar Rapids Lock & Key Service, 3217 1st Avenue SE, 52402, (319-365-5162); **Grinnel,** Larry A. Sheets, 626 East Street, 50112, (515-236-6325); **Indianola,** Herb Dunn Jr., Metal Detector Sales, Route 4, 50125, (515-981-4341); **Larrabee,** Ray's Winchesters & Coins, Main Street, 51029, (712-437-2205); **Tama,** McGrew Oil Co., 120 W. 4th Street, 52339, (515-484-2946, 489-2396); **Waterloo,** Dean Boyd, 1047 Evergreen, 50701, (319-232-9484); **Waverly,** Trading Post, 403 West Bremer, Box 251, 50677, (319-352-9874 or 352-2942).

KANSAS: Belleville, Kesl's Jewelry and Sporting Goods, 1800 M Street, 66935, (913-527-5193); **Dodge City,** Carl Clare, 911 3rd Avenue, 66801, (316-225-5005 or 225-4701); **Manhattan,** Radio Shack Associate Store, 2609 Anderson Avenue, 66502, (913-539-6151); **Pratt,** Epp's Coin Shop, 112 S. Main Street, 67124, (316-672-6181, 672-6277); **Sedan,** El Dorado Detectors, 407 N. Hooper Street, 67361, (316-725-3784); **South Hutchinson,** Armstrong Detectors, 117 Forest, 67505, (316-665-8693); **Topeka,** Maxine's Treasure Sales, 5425 SW Wanamaker Road, 66604, (913-862-2872); **Wichita,** Swaim Electronics, 1430 E. Douglas, 67214, (316-262-0077).

KENTUCKY: Ashland, Gambill Lock & Electronics, 1004 Comanche Ct., 41101, (606-325-7931); **Louisville,** A. F. Waller, P. O. Box 72083, 40272, (502-937-8008); **Nicholasville,** Paul Phillips, 109 Lake Street, 40356, (606-885-3648).

LOUISIANA: Benton, A-Able Treasure Electronics, 102 Duval, 71006, (318-965-0277); **Baton Rouge,** Confederate States Metal Detector Sales, 2905 Government Street, 70806, (504-387-5044); J & F Enterprises, 12211 Greenwell Springs Road, 70814, (504-272-8500); **Many,** The Sabine Index, 850 San Antonio Avenue, 71449, (318-256-3495); **Metairie,** Henry L. Montegut, 437 Aurora Avenue, 70005, (504-834-2378).

MARYLAND: Baltimore, Codi Treasure Outfitters, 408 South High Street, 21202, (301-837-9387); Treasure Detectors of Maryland, 4069 Beach Road, 21222, (301-477-8827); **Edgewater,** Finders Keepers, John Reichenberg, Route 4, 3316 Oak Drive, 21037, (301-798-1833); **Glenburnie,** Frank's Detectors of Glenburnie, 408 Arbor Drive, 21061, (301-768-3157); **Westover,** Somco Machine Co., Route 1, Box 272, 21871, (301-651-1516, 651-3964).

MASSACHUSETTS: Agawam, E & D Electronic Sales & Service, 83 Parker Street, 01001, (413-786-7190); **Auburn,** Found Enterprises, 65 Auburn Street, 01501, (617-832-3721); **Haverhill,** Gold Key Detector, 62 Crystal Street, 01830, (617-373-0004); **Rehoboth,** Larry Violette, Box 74, 02769, (617-252-4497); **W. Springfield,** A. J. Dumais, Dumais Electronics Corporation, 37 Spring Street, 01089, (413-733-9548).

MICHIGAN: Bay City, Buzzard's Metal Detector Sales, 1724 E. Salzburg Rd., 48706, (517-684-4765); **Dearborn,** Raymond R. Huffmaster Electronics, 1537 Monroe, 48124, (313-278-7922, 278-1940); **Grand Rapids,** Grant's Book Store, 601 Bridge Street NW, 49504, (616-458-6580); **Lansing,** Finders Keepers Metal Detectors, 2112 Cumberland Road, 48906, (517-321-6594, 323-4250); **Union Lake,** Old Prospectors Shack, 7007 Cooley Lake Road, 48085, (313-363-7328); **Wyoming,** Treasure Hunter's Supply, 3930 Burlingame SW, 49509, (616-538-1957).

MINNESOTA: Bloomington, Mid-West Metal Detectors, 8338 Pillsbury Avenue So., 55420, (612-881-5254); **Minneapolis,** Garrett Metal Detector Specialists, 3249 Nicollet Avenue S, 55408, (612-827-3113); **St. Paul,** Minnesota Prospectors Supply, Formerly of Red Wing, MN, 902 Goodrich, 55105, (612-226-5118); **Walhalla,** Schillings, 136 Fair Oaks, 49458, (616-757-2912); **White Pine,** Wayne's A&E Service Center, 20 Maple Street, 49971, (906-885-5543).

MISSISSIPPI: Gautier, Treasure Island, 1439 Hallmark Plaza, 39553, (601-497-5651); **Jackson,** Eagle Arms Co., 3115 Terry Rd., 39212, (601-373-4557); **Tupelo,** Hobbies Unlimited, P. O. Box 1161, 1219 Nelle Street, 38801, (601-842-6031).

MISSOURI: Aurora, Aurora Detector Sales & Valuables Recovery Service, 303 Rock Street, 65605, (417-678-2902); **California,** Twin City Gun & CB, 500 Cooper Street, 65018, (314-796-2166); **Florissant,** The Prospector's Shack, 975 Grenoble Lane, 63033, (314-837-4703); **Fredericktown,** Allen's Hobby Shop, Court Square, 63645, (314-783-5500); **Hillsboro,** E & R Detector Sales, P. O. Box 213, 63050, (314-789-2078, 586-4263); **Independence,** Ozark Treasure Chest, 1816 Ellison, 64050, (816-252-8998); **Joplin,** Frank's Sales & Service, Route 3, Box 834, 64801, (417-781-6597); **Kansas City,** Clevengers Detector Sales, 8206 North Oak Street Trfwy., 64118, (816-436-0697); **Poplar Bluff,** The Treasure Hut, 1315 North Main, 63901, (314-785-1164); **Springfield,** Radford Jewelers, 1864 South Glenstone, 65804, (417-881-7308); **Ste. Genevieve,** Kreilich TV, RR#1, 63670, (314-883-2070); **St. Joseph,** Stanley Johnson Co., 2607 So. 14th, 64503, (816-232-5163);

St. Louis, Plateau Detector Center, 9837 Kimker, 63127, (314-842-0413); **Sullivan,** John's Metal Detector Sales, 250 E. Euclid, 63080, (314-468-6208).

MONTANA: Missoula, Electronic Parts, 1030 S. Avenue West, P. O. Box 2126, 59801, (406-543-3119); **Ronan,** Western Seed & Supply Inc., Box 67 Old Highway 93, 59864, (406-676-4100).

NEBRASKA: Ames, Exanimo Establishment, Main Street, 68621, (402-727-9833, 721-9438); **Sprague,** L. P. Enterprises, Box 46, 1420 W. 3rd Street, 68438, (402-794-5730).

NEVADA: Carson City, Gold Prospector's Supply, 1441 Rand Avenue, 89701, (702-883-8444); **Fallon,** Scott Goodpasture, 9525 Pioneer Way, 89406, (702-867-2015); **Reno,** Sierra Detectors, 419 Flint, 89501, (702-323-2712); Len Fuhr Enterprises, 1260 Brinkby Avenue, 89509, (702-827-2311).

NEW HAMPSHIRE: Concord, Don Wilson Sales, 93 So. State Street, 03301, (603-224-5909); **Seabrook,** The Village Trader, U. S. Route 1, 03874, (603-474-2836).

NEW JERSEY: Englewood, General Sales, #10 Humphrey Street, 07631, (201-568-5563); **Saddle Brook,** Geo-Quest, 104 US Hwy. 46, 07662, (201-772-7443); **Trenton,** Treasure Cove, 1055 S. Clinton Avenue, 08611, (609-393-3631, 989-7382).

NEW MEXICO: Albuquerque, Kohl's Rock Shop, 928 Eubank NE, 87112, (505-298-6536); **Aztec,** Wooley's Trailer Sales, 635 Aztec Boulevard, 87410, (505-334-2871); **Roswell,** Roswell Treasure Center, #12 Monterey Shopping Center, 1400 West Second Street, 88201, (505-623-2242); **Santa Fe,** Manos De Plata De Santa Fe, 1023 Bishops Lodge Road, 87501, (505-982-2872).

NEW YORK: Catskill, Freds Bike & Canoe, RD 1, Box 358, 12414, (518-943-2173); **Fairport,** Lost Coins Enterprise, Darrell K. Kilburn, 721 Mosley Rd., 14450, (716-223-2139); **Fayettville,** Roman E. Fedyk, 5100 Highbridge Street Suite 36D, 13066, (315-637-3031); **Geneva,** J. Panna's Electronic Sales, P. O. Box 167, 14456, (315-789-0809); **Glen Cove,** Fred Bond, 2 Leech Circle So., 11542, (516-676-1310); **Manhattan,** Louie Calamia, 54 East 8th Street, 10003, (212-254-1763); **New York City,** C-T Detectors, 4443 Murdock Avenue, 10466, (212-325-9542); **Syracuse,** Jerrys Treasure Den, 1208 Milton Avenue, 13204, (315-468-3615); **Walton,** Doc Dave's Treasure Finders, 54 Stockton Avenue, Route 206, 13856, (607-865-5188).

NORTH CAROLINA: Asheboro, Treasure World of North Carolina, East Dixie Drive, 27203, (919-629-6164); **Asheville,** Strings & Things, 1064 Patton Avenue, 28806, (704-258-3589); **Bladenboro,** Miller Electronics, Route 2, Box 744, 28320, (919-866-5600); **Charlotte,** Ernie "Carolina" Curlee, Detector Sales Co., Division of Chemation, 3201 Cullman Avenue, 28206, (704-375-8468, 537-5115); **Glen Raven,** Barbee Detector Sales, c/o Barbee Fabrics, Inc., P. O. Box 4235, 27215, (919-584-7781, 584-7873); **Moncure,** B & R Detector Sales, Route 1, Box 185-D, 27559, (919-542-2210, 542-3832); **Wilmington,** Russ Simmons, 414 Biscayne Drive, 28405, (919-686-7059).

NORTH DAKOTA: Fargo, Treasure Island, West Acres Shopping Center, 58103, (701-282-4747); **Minot,** Chester N. Iverson, 808 17th Avenue S.W., 58701, (701-838-0149).

OHIO: Ashtabula, McCoy Electronic Repair, 7830 Sanborn Road, 44004, (216-997-4050); **Chillicothe,** Jack B. Eley, 308 Plyleys Lane, 45601, (614-772-2767); **Cincinnatti,** J & B Treasures (Northwest Accessories), 2163 Sevenshills Drive, 45240, (513-742-3344); Treasure Hunters Supplies, 1501 Clovernoll Drive, 45231, (513-729-2084 or 521-0678); **Cleveland,** Kilian Detector Equipment Company, 1031 Spring Road, 44109, (216-398-4779); **Elyria,** T & K Cycles, 36668 Butternut Ridge Rd., 44035, (216-327-3783); **Greenville,** Midwest, 509 South Broadway, 45331, (513-548-5970); **Lewisburg,** Fox Metal Detectors, Shields Road, RR #2, Box 312 D, 45338, (513-962-2937); **Lima,** Klingler's Rocks 'N Things, 1763 Bowman Road, 45804, (419-227-5294); **Marion,** Marion Electronics Dist., 698-708 North Main Street, 43302, (614-382-0913); **Millersport,** The Penny Place, P.O. Box 578, 3163 North Street, 43046, (614-467-2864); **Oregonia,** Fort Ancient Trading Post, 5277 Rt 350, 6 miles East on Lebanon, 45054, (513-932-3109); **Ottawa,** Winkle Radio & TV, Route 4, 17 Mi. N. Lima, 1½ Mi. N. Kalida, Route 115, 45875, (419-532-3957); **Pierpont,** G & D Detector Sales, 6500 North Richmond Road, 44082, (216-577-1496); **Shelby,** Struble Drug Inc. of Shelby, 31 West Main Street, 44875, (419-342-2136, 347-2802); **Toledo,** National Camper Sales, 7417 West Central, 43617, (419-841-2444); The Treasure House, 5734 Elmer, 43615, (419-531-7787); **Waterville,** The Treasure Chest, 3 Mi. W. Waterville, Route 24, 9204 S. River Road, 43566, (419-878-6026).

OKLAHOMA: Ada, Eddie S. Fausett Sales, 2729 Kirby Drive, 74820, (405-332-3156); **Dewey,** F & M Detector Sales, 902 East 7th Street, 74029, (918-534-2382); **Keota,** James Bruner & Sons, Route One, 74941, (918-966-3779); **Maud,** Dewey's Phillips 66 Service Station, 301 West King Street, 74854, (405-374-2786); **Okeene,** Jim A. Pavlu, Rt. 2 Box 118A, 73763, (405-822-4810); **Okemah,** Territory Town U.S.A., Rt. 2 Box 297 A, 74859, (918-623-9933); **Oklahoma City,** Hobby World, 2433 Plaza Prom, Shepherd Mall, 73107, (405-942-4556); **Tulsa,** Ace's Detector Service, 5622 S. Pittsburg, 74135, (918-742-2214); **Turpin,** Joe Lawder, RR #1, Box 22, 73950, (405-854-6429).

OREGON: Coos Bay, Carla Kay Salvage Co., 471 Brule Street, 97420, (503-888-4015); **Eugene,** Oregon Gold Dredge Limited, P.O. Box 10214, 50 Grimes Road, 97440, (503-686-2769); **Grant's Pass,** Kelly Metalcraft, 5057 Redwood Avenue, 97526, (503-479-1767); **Portland,** D & K Detector Sales, 13809 SE Division, 97236, (503-761-1521).

PENNSYLVANIA: Boothwyn, American Odyssey, Garrett Metal Detectors, 2612 Chichester Avenue, 19061, (215-485-3011); **Gettysburg,** Gettysburg Electronics, 24 Chambersburg Street, 17325, (717-334-8634); **Greensburg,** Sealand's Metal Detectors, 422 Sells Lane, 15601, (412-834-3429); **Johnstown,** J & D Metal Locating Equip., RD 6, 15909, (814-749-9411 or 322-4984); **Meadville,** Miller's Treasure & Metal Detectors, RD #1, Pettis Rd., 16335, (814-336-5453); **Milford,** Warren Pedersen, RR 2, Box 381, 18337, (717-296-7285); **Morrisdale,** Robert & Cleora Ferguson, P.O. Box 14, Route 53, 16858, (814-342-1268); **New Castle,** Barker Advertising, RD #5 Mitchell Road, 16105, (412-652-7596); **Williamsport,** K. A. Detectors, RD 4, Box 323, 17701, (717-326-0867).

RHODE ISLAND: Warwick, House of Bargains, 345 Warwick Avenue, 02888, (401-781-8580).

SOUTH CAROLINA: Sumter, Ken Lyles Detectors, 122 Lazy Lane, 29150, (803-775-8840 or 773-9577).

SOUTH DAKOTA: Rapid City, Donco Metal Detectors, 2424 Canyon Lake Drive, 57701, (605-343-3103).

TENNESSEE: Bolivar, West Tennessee Detector Sales, 322 Central Street, P.O. Box 162, 38008, (901-658-5196); **Chattanooga,** Chattanooga Detector Sales, 3110 3rd Avenue, 37407, (615-622-8882); **Chattanooga,** Hickory Valley Electric Co. and Metal Detector Sales, 6916 Lee Hwy., 37421, (615-892-0525, 892-3581); **Memphis,** Memphis Numismatics, Inc., 11 South Orleans Street, 38103, (901-526-5054); Mid-South Metal Detector Sales, 3190 Summer Avenue, 38112, (901-452-8860); **Nashville,** The Collector's Shop, 100 Oaks Shopping Center, 37204, (615-383-5996); **Selmer,** Selmer Service Station & Sporting Goods, 100 West Court Avenue, 38375, (901-645-5431).

TEXAS: Amarillo, J. C. Claxton, 1602 Canyon Drive, 79102, 806-373-8971, 374-3820); **Austin,** Niles Carter, 2103 Whitestone Drive, 78745, (512-444-0106); **Beaumont,** Sanders Sports Shop, Route 8, Box G-36, 77705, (713-794-2560); **Brownsville,** Chester's Coin Shop, 2606 International Blvd., 78521, (512-546-4252); **Bryan,** Treasure Hound Detector Sales, 400 Mitchell, 77801, (713-779-6423, 845-2211); **Corpus Christi,** Bayside Metal Detectors, 9245 So. Padre Island Drive, 78418, (512-937-1682, 937-5334); **Dallas,** United Treasure Hunters, 11602 Garland Road, 75218, (214-328-4327 or 328-1223); **Donna,** E. David Medrano, 410 So. 23rd Street, 78537, (512-464-4270); **Dublin,** Cross Timbers Search Electronics, 831 Preston Lane, 76346, (817-445-2337); **El Paso,** American Camping & Outing Industries, Inc., P. O. Box 12564, 79912, (915-751-7741); **Ft. Worth,** Gray's, 1601 West Berry Street, 76110, (817-921-2431); Rex Grove Auto Supply Co., Inc., 4527 E. Belknap, 76117, (817-838-3066, 838-9640); **Harlingen,** Green Gables — Metal Detector Sales, 1910 N "77" Sunshine, 78550, (512-428-8420); **Houston,** Alexander Enterprises, 21 Spencer Highway, 77587, (713-946-6399); **Houston,** Research & Recovery, 2803 Old Spanish Trail, 77054, (713-747-4647, 747-4648); **Jacksonville,** Piney Woods Market, Box 1722 Lake Springs Road, 75766, (214-586-2448); **Kerrville,** Hill Country Detectors, 10 Donna Drive, 78028, (512-257-4760); **Manvel,** The Treasure Hunter, Box 558, 77578, (713-489-9156); **Mesquite,** Search & Recovery, Rt. 1 Box 185-B, 75181, (214-222-8322); **Mission,** Mission Rexall Drug, 1030 Conway Avenue, 78572, (512-585-1532); **San Antonio,** Owens Detector Sales, 5814 Kepler Drive, 78228, (512-434-1605); **Texas City,** Treasure Hunters Supply, 1819 6th Street North (Loop 197), 77590, (713-948-8312); **Uvalde,** Spurgeon's Artifacts & Coins, 205 W. Nueces, 78801, (512-278-2164); **Wichita Falls,** Jerry Eckhart's Southwestern Treasure Outfitters, 4226 Old Jacksboro Highway, 76302, (817-767-3939).

UTAH: Bountiful, Pat Blackner's House of Treasure, 581 West 800 South, 84010, (801-292-3111); **Roy,** Bryant T. Cash, 2457 West 4975 South, 84067, (801-825-7858).

VIRGINIA: Fairfax, Suburban Detectors. 3169 Spring Street, 22031, (703-273-2542); **Richmond,** Essential Electronics, 10453 Medina Rd., 23235, (804-272-5558); **Virginia Beach,** H & S Detector Center, 2108 Thoroughpond Rd., 23455, (804-464-6072).

WASHINGTON: Auburn, Cache Inn Detectors, 17925 S.E. 313th, 98002, (206-631-0466); **Bellingham,** Washington Divers, 903 N. State Street, 98225, (206-676-8029); **Bremerton,** Tanner's Diggin's, 4029 Boundary Trail NW, 98310, (206-830-4544); **Cle Elum,** Blackfeather's Liberty Cafe, Blewett Pass Highway, 98922, (509-857-9393); **Kennewick,** The Coin Cradle Inc., 2810 W. Kennewick Avenue, Suite "E", 99336, (509-735-1507); **Seattle,** Pearl Electronics Inc., 1300 First Avenue, 98101, (206-622-6200); Prospector Ed's Gold Supplies, 5263 Rainier Avenue So., 98118, (206-723-8200); **Spokane,** Bowen's Hideout, S. 1823 Mt. Vernon, 99203, (509-534-4004).

WISCONSIN: Blackriver Falls, Indian Head Recoveries, RR 1, Box 117, 54615, (715-284-2105); **Kenosha,** Franks, 4525 Wilson Road, 53142, (414-654-1764); **Madison,** Pete's Rock Shop, 1917-19 Winnebago Street, 53704, (608-249-2648); **Menomouee Falls,** Dons Treasure Hunting Supply, N88 W16747 Appleton Avenue, 53051 (414-251-5350); **Milwaukee,** Casanova's, 1601 West Greenfield Avenue, 53204, (414-672-3040); **Sheboygan,** Jetzer's Metal Detector Sales, 3212 North 21st Street, 53081, (414-457-9231); **Waukesha,** Outdoor Outfitters, 705 Elm Ct., 53186, (414-542-7772).

WEST VIRGINIA: Morgantown, Ideal Home Entertainment Center Inc., 733 Fairmont Road, 26505, (304-292-7301); **Paden City,** Murdock's Hobby Shop, 121 North Fourth Avenue, 26159, (304-337-2711); **Shady Spring,** Ray's Leisure Time Shop, P. O. Drawer E, US Highways, 19 & 21, 25918, (304-763-3110).

WYOMING: Casper, Caspar Metal Detectors Sales & Rentals, 1281 Payne and 1017 Cardiff, 82601, (307-235-6323, 234-5205).

FOREIGN

AUSTRALIA, Victoria, Park, P. J. Bridge Hesperian Detectors, P. O. Box 317, 6100, Western Australia, (09-32-57422, 32-58575.

CANADA
ALBERTA: Edmonton, Bedrock Detectors, 10250-82 Street, T6A 3M3, (403-469-3050); **Milk River,** Jerry's Detectors, P.O. Box 536, 508-4th Avenue N.E., TOK 1T0, (403-647-3851); **Rocky Mountain House,** Discovery Detectors, Box 1284, T0M 1T0, (403-845-3718).

BRITISH COLUMBIA, Vancouver, Diversified Electronics Limited, 1104 Franklin Street, V6A 1J6, (604-254-0761).

MANITOBA; Winnipeg, O. K. John, Stn. F. Box 54, R2L 2A5; (204-667-6556).

NEW BRUNSWICK: Stanley, York Carleton, Treasure Supplies, P.O. Box 147, EOH 1T0, (506-367-2955).

ONTARIO: *Canadian Treasure Trail Ltd., P. O. Box 22, Camden East, K0K 1J0, (613-378-6421) *Distributor and Service Center for Canada; **Ayr,** Treasure Unlimited, Box 257, NOB 1E0, (519-632-7955); **Downsview,** Sub-Mariners Diving Equipment, 954 Wilson Avenue, M3K 1E7, (416-630-2590); **Peterborough,** Leisure Detector Sales, Box 44, K9J 6Y5, (705-745-7655); **Scarborough,** Pirates Cove, 3274 Danforth Avenue, M1L 1C3, (416-691-5560); **Stirling,** Tall Pines Treasure Trail, Box 186, (613-395-2406); **Strathroy,** L. W. Electronics, Box 42, (519-245-1994). **Waterford,** D. Keith Edwards, RR #5, NOE 1Y0, (519-443-5193).

SASKATCHEWAN: Fort Qu'Appelle, Ken Co Industries, P.O. Box 280, SOG 1S0, (332-5312). **Yorkton,** John Menken, 67 Darlington Street E., S3N 0C4, (306-783-8336).

CARIBBEAN AREA INCLUDING INCL — CENTRAL & SOUTH AMERICA
FLORIDA: Maitland, Bourne International, 512 Oak Lane, 32751, (305-645-4563).
VENEZUELA: Caracas, Victor Alvarez, P.O. Box 60705, 1060, (72-83-20).

AFRICA
SOUTH AFRICA: Overport Durban, DECO, P.O. Box 37606, 4067, (031-336409).

GREAT BRITAIN & IRELAND
ENGLAND: London, *Pieces of Eight, 259 Eversholt Street, N.W.1, (01-388-3686) *Distributor and Service Center for UK, **London,** Treasure World, 155 Robert Street, N.W.1, (01-387-3142).

MEXICO
CALIFORNIA: San Diego, Gem & Treasure Hunting Association, 2493 San Diego Avenue, 92110, (714-297-2672) (Closed Monday & Tuesday).

TEXAS: Donna, E. David Medrano, 410 So. 23rd Street, 78537, (512-464-4270).

PUERTO RICO: Caparra Terrace-Rio Piedras, Treasure Hunting Center, 1572 Jesus T. Pinero Avenue, 00921, (809-781-6902).

RECOMMENDED SUPPLEMENTARY BOOKS

The books described below are among the most popular books in print related to treasure hunting. If you desire to increase your skills in various aspects of treasure hunting, consider adding these volumes to your library.

DETECTOR OWNER'S FIELD MANUAL. Roy Lagal. Ram Publishing Company. Nowhere else will you find the detector operating instructions that Mr. Lagal has put into this book. He shows in detail how to treasure hunt, cache hunt, prospect, search for nuggets, black sand deposits ... in short, how to use your detector exactly as it should be used. Covers completely BFO-TR-VLF/TR types, P.I.'s, P.R.G.'s, P.I.P's, etc. Explains precious metals, minerals, ground conditions, and gives proof that treasure exists because it has been found and that more exists that you can find! Fully illustrated. 236 pages. $6.95.

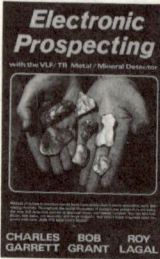

ELECTRONIC PROSPECTING. Charles Garrett, Bob Grant, Roy Lagal. Ram Publishing Company. A tremendous upswing in electronic prospecting for gold and other precious metals has recently occurred. High gold prices and unlimited capabilities of VLF/TR metal detectors have led to many fantastic discoveries. Gold is there to be found. If you have the desire to search for it and want to be successful, then this book will show you how to select (and use) from the many brands of VLF/TR's those that are correctly calibrated to produce accurate metal vs. mineral identification which is so vitally necessary in prospecting. Illustrated. 96 pages. $3.95.

GOLD PANNING IS EASY. Roy Lagal. Ram Publishing Company. Roy Lagal proves it! He doesn't introduce a new method; he removes confusion surrounding old established methods. A refreshing NEW LOOK guaranteed to produce results with the "Gravity Trap" or any other pan. Special metal detector instructions that show you how to nugget shoot, find gold and silver veins, and check ore samples for precious metal. This HOW, WHERE and WHEN gold panning book is a must for everyone, beginner or professional! Fully illustrated. 96 pages. $3.95.

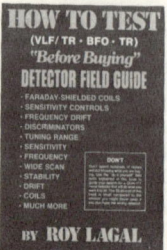

HOW TO TEST "BEFORE BUYING" DETECTOR FIELD GUIDE. Roy Lagal. Ram Publishing Company. Completely explains the inner workings of the BFO, TR, and discriminator types of detectors. You will learn how to test for sensitivity, stability, total response, wide scan, soil conditions, coils, Faraday shields, and frequency drift, and you will be able to expose incompetent detector engineering and overly enthusiastic, misleading advertising. If you own or are thinking of buying a detector, this book is an ABSOLUTE MUST. Fully illustrated. 64 pages. $3.95.

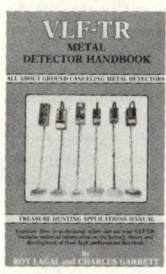

THE COMPLETE VLF-TR METAL DETECTOR HANDBOOK (All About Ground Canceling Metal Detectors). Roy Lagal, Charles Garrett. Ram Publishing Company. The unparalleled capabilities of VLF/TR Ground Canceling metal detectors have made them the number one choice of treasure hunters and prospectors. From History, Theory, and Development to Coin, Cache, and Relic Hunting, as well as Prospecting, the authors have explained in detail the capabilities of VLF/TR detectors and how they are used. Learn the new ground canceling detectors for the greatest possible success. Illustrated. 200 pages. $7.95.

THE JOURNALS OF EL DORADO. Estee Conatser, Karl von Mueller. Ram Publishing Company. A descriptive bibliography on treasure and related subjects; a first-of-its-kind storehouse of information devoted exclusively to information of interest to treasure hunters, prospectors, and relic hunters. This book contains approximately 1,800 book listings arranged alphabetically by author. It was developed as a working tool and reference for those in the treasure, small mining, and prospecting fields, especially beginners. Thousands of treasure leads will be found between its covers. Invaluable. 380 pages. $9.95.

TREASURE HUNTER'S MANUAL #6. Karl von Mueller. Ram Publishing Company. The original material in this book was written for the professional treasure hunter. Hundreds of copies were paid for in advance by professionals who knew the value of Karl's writing and wanted no delays in receiving their copies. The THM #6 completely describes full-time treasure hunting and explains the mysteries surrounding this intriguing and rewarding field of endeavor. You'll read this fascinating book several times. Each time you will discover you have gained greater in-depth knowledge. Thousands of ideas, tips, and other valuable information. Illustrated. 318 pages. $7.95.

TREASURE HUNTER'S MANUAL #7. Karl von Mueller. Ram Publishing Company. The classic! The most complete, up-to-date guide to America's fastest growing activity, written by the old master of treasure hunting. This is *the* book that fully describes professional methods of RESEARCH, RECOVERY, and TREASURE DISPOSITION. Includes a full range of treasure hunting methods from research techniques to detector operation, from legality to gold dredging. Don't worry that this material overlaps THM #6 ... both of Karl's MANUALS are 100% different from each other but yet are crammed with information you should know about treasure hunting. Illustrated. 334 pages. $7.95.

 **SUCCESSFUL COIN HUNTING.** Charles Garrett. Ram Publishing Company. The best and most complete guide to successful coin hunting, this book explains fully the how's, where's, and when's of searching for coins and related objects. It also includes a complete explanation of how to select and use the various types of coin hunting metal detectors. Based on more than twenty years of actual in-the-field experience by the author, this volume contains a great amount of practical coin hunting information that will not be found elsewhere. Profusely illustrated with over 100 photographs. 248 pages. $6.95.

 **TREASURE HUNTING PAYS OFF!** Charles Garrett. Ram Publishing Company. This book will give you an excellent introduction to all facets of treasure hunting. It tells you how to begin and be successful in general treasure hunting; coin hunting; relic, cache, and bottle seeking; and prospecting. It describes the various kinds of metal/mineral detectors and tells you how to go about selecting the correct type for all kinds of searching. This is an excellent guidebook for the beginner, but yet contains tips and ideas for the experienced TH'er Illustrated. 92 pages. $3.95

 **THE COMPLETE BOOK OF COMPETITION TREASURE HUNTING.** Ernie "Carolina" Curlee. Ram Publishing Company. This book gives the details you need to know to sponsor or compete successfully in an organized treasure hunt. All about everything from choosing a name for a hunt and promoting it to receiving the prize you may have won. Whole sections on "How To Sponsor" and "How To Win." Every metal detector owner/treasure hunter can benefit from Ernie's down-to-earth, plainly written information and instructions. A book that will pay for itself many times over! Fully illustrated. 88 pages. $5.95.

 **PROFESSIONAL TREASURE HUNTER.** George Mroczkowski. Ram Publishing Company. Research is 90 percent of the success of any treasure hunting endeavor. You will become a better treasure hunter by learning how, through proper treasure hunting techniques and methods, George was able to find treasure sites, obtain permission to search (even from the U. S. Government), select and use the proper equipment, and then recover treasure in many instances. If treasure was not found, valuable clues and historical artifacts were located that made it worthwhile or kept the search alive. Profusely illustrated. 132 pages. $6.95.

SPECIAL PUBLICATIONS OF THE
International Treasure Hunting Society

The International Treasure Hunting Society (ITHS) publishes a quarterly journal, THE INTERNATIONAL TREASURE HUNTER. Each issue contains carefully selected "how to" information regarding treasure hunting, metal detecting, prospecting, relic hunting, and other projects, as well as the latest successful treasure hunting stories of treasures found world-wide. Other information about treasure-hunting clubs and competition treasure hunts is also included. Copies are distributed free to ITHS members. Non-members may purchase one or more publications from Ram Publishing Company for $1.50 each. Copies may also be ordered direct from ITHS, P.O. Box 3007, Garland, Texas 75041. Obtain information about ITHS by writing the same address or by calling 214-271-0800.

THE INTERNATIONAL TREASURE HUNTER, Vol. 1, No. 1. This premier issue contains complete information regarding the organization and founding of the ITHS. Several informative articles include, "Electronic Treasure Hunting: The First Fifty Years," "Europe: A Treasure Hunter's Paradise!," and "The Soldier's Legacy, Searching for Battlefield Relics." These are but three of the articles included in this first issue which has now become a collector's item. $1.50 each.

THE INTERNATIONAL TREASURE HUNTER, Vol. 2, No. 1. This second issue has numerous "how to" articles, including a special coin hunting article by famed treasure hunter T. R. Edds. Read this article to learn how to "Unlock Ocean Beach Treasure Vaults." Other special articles tell about gold hunting in Australia, the First International Championship Treasure Hunt, and the first treasure hunter to search the ghost town of Spring Creek, Colorado. There are many other articles. $1.50 each.

THE INTERNATIONAL TREASURE HUNTER, Vol. 2, No. 2, Special articles about mystery money found in Texas, hunting ghost sites, underwater detecting, and a very successful lady treasure hunter spark this issue of ITH. Regular features on treasure clubs, public service, relic hunting, and book reviews continue to keep treasure hunters up-to-date on happenings in their hobby. This issue also includes announcement of a new film about prospecting and several treasure hunting tips. Don't miss it! Limited quantity. $1.50 each.

BOOK ORDER BLANK

See your detector dealer or bookstore or send check or money order directly to Ram for prompt, postage paid shipping. If not completely satisfied return book(s) within 10 days for a full refund.

- ___ DETECTOR OWNER'S FIELD MANUAL **$6.95**
- ___ ELECTRONIC PROSPECTING **$3.95**
- ___ GOLD PANNING IS EASY **$3.95**
- ___ HOW TO TEST "BEFORE BUYING" DETECTOR FIELD GUIDE **$3.95**
- ___ COMPLETE VLF-TR METAL DETECTOR HANDBOOK (THE) (ALL ABOUT GROUND CANCELING METAL DETECTORS) **7.95**
- ___ JOURNALS OF EL DORADO (THE) **$9.95**
- ___ TREASURE HUNTER'S MANUAL #6 **$7.95**
- ___ TREASURE HUNTER'S MANUAL #7 **$7.95**
- ___ SUCCESSFUL COIN HUNTING **$6.95**
- ___ TREASURE HUNTING PAYS OFF! **$3.95**
- ___ COMPLETE BOOK OF COMPETITION TREASURE HUNTING (THE) **$5.95**
- ___ PROFESSIONAL TREASURE HUNTER **$6.95**
- ___ INTERNATIONAL TREASURE HUNTER, Vol. 1, No.1 **$1.50**
- ___ INTERNATIONAL TREASURE HUNTER Vol. 2, No.1 **$1.50**
- ___ INTERNATIONAL TREASURE HUNTER Vol. 2, No. 2 **$1.50**

Please add 35¢ for each book ordered (to a maximum of $1.00) for handling charges.

Total for Items	$ _____
Texas Residents Add 5% State Tax	_____
Handling Charge	_____
Total of Above	$ _____

ENCLOSED IS MY CHECK OR MONEY ORDER $ _____

NAME _____

ADDRESS _____

CITY _____

STATE _____ ZIP _____

PLACE MY NAME ON YOUR MAILING LIST ☐

Ram Publishing Company
P.O. Drawer 38649, Dallas, Texas 75238
Dept. TH5
214-278-8439
DEALER INQUIRIES WELCOME